Praise for Dear Dad

"A story of trial. A story of pain. A story of hope. A story of gritty redemption."

—Suzette Brawner, author and speaker

"Sundi Jo's collection of letters to her father is an intensely intimate glimpse into her heart; a heart that dramatically changes throughout the journal writing. Her outpouring of raw emotion lends a uniquely compelling authenticity to her story. Her wide-open honesty reveals a candid depiction of brokenness resulting from a life filled with abuse and self-doubt. Sundi Jo's relentless search for hope and meaning unfolds as a healing story of forgiveness, of release from the past that held her captive, and of victory experienced in surrender. I found myself joining her along this journey, cheering her onward as her heart gradually softened toward others and especially herself while taking steps toward surrendering her life to her Lord and Savior, Jesus Christ. Truly inspiring! The powerful transformation in Sundi Jo's heart and her desire to serve God and others is certain to change lives. Sundi Jo's dad would be so very proud of her."

—Mary Beth Carlson, Songwriter,
performing and recording artist, author
and inspirational speaker

"This gut-wrenchingly honest journey of addiction to restoration in Jesus will leave you unable to put this book down. The author's unflinchingly raw account of moving from abuse, rebellion, addiction and confusion to healing will move you. As I turned each page with ever-increasing urgency, desperate to find out how her story ends, I couldn't help but silently cheer her on.

This book is important, particularly for anyone who has suffered and is feeling confused, lost and alone. What becomes abundantly clear is that Jesus is the true author of her life, freely giving grace, healing, forgiveness and redemption. Sundi Jo's life is now a shining example of how Jesus can turn any broken life into a brand new one, full of hope.

Ultimately, this story is one of compassion. It is a reminder to treat all people with love and kindness, rather than judgment. It's a reminder that people are struggling with all kinds of problems, often in silence, and that Jesus would have us offer the branch of gentle hope than of stern criticism."

—Julie Cave, Author of
The Dinah Harris Series

Sundi Jo holds nothing back. I admire her straightforward, straight to the heart approach to life, ministry and this book. *Dear Dad* gives hope to the lost. If you have ever struggled with your identity, read this book. You will be greatly encouraged in your walk with Christ.

—Ted Cunningham
Pastor and Author, *Young and
In Love* and *Trophy Child*

"Broken. Confused. Drugs. Alcohol. Sex. Abuse. Obesity. Anger. Fear. In this compelling book, Sundi Jo opens her heart and shares her journey from a life of emptiness and pain to a life that now knows the peace and joy of a personal relationship with Jesus. *Dear Dad* will move you to tears, grip your heart, and cause you to look at your own walk with the Lord. After reading *Dear Dad* it will be impossible for your life to ever be the same! Sundi Jo shows us the beautiful transformation that takes place when we become a true follower of Christ."

—Clara Hinton, author of *Silent Grief*

It's been said that most stories are about a son searching for a father. But this is a book about a Father finding his daughter — and the yearning we all have to be found and fathered well. Sundi Jo's story will wound you, heal you, and help you see your story in light of a larger narrative.

—Jeff Goins, author, Wrecked: When a Broken World Slams into Your Comfortable Life

Sundi Jo is my hero. Reading "Dear Dad" is like reading a secret diary full of pain and brokenness with a heavy shot of redemption. Her story resonates with me in so many ways. We have so much in common and the best thing we share is that we have both been redeemed. She is so authentic about her battle scars and pain. The wounds she suffered as a child shaped her future in detrimental ways. She is a miracle to have overcome so much!! She continually offers hope and sends the reader to the merciful heart of Jesus. I wept reading this book, remembering each moment where God gave me beauty for ashes. You will be blessed in the reading and more blessed by her heart yielded in complete surrender to the Savior who set her free! "Dear Dad" is powerfully written, practically helpful and offers deep healing. This is a must read for anyone who has ever been hurt or broken. I am certain this book will be a powerful tool used to bring healing to wounded hearts all over the world.

—Tammy Bolt Werthem, life coach, author

Sundi Jo's sincere and well-written story, Dear Dad, perfectly exemplifies what I've found to be true in my nearly twenty years of medical practice. Unless we deal with it directly, emotional and spiritual pain can translate into physical illness and addictive, self-destructive behavior. Kudos to Sundi Jo for bravely seeking God's healing truth and restoration. And double-kudos to her for putting her story in writing so that others can benefit.

—Dr. Rita Hancock, M.D., author, Radical
Well-being

With each letter in Dear Dad I could feel Sundi Jo becoming more and more free and finding that stillness within that we all long for. Sundi Jo's raw authentic transparency in "Dear Dad" captivated me and I couldn't stop reading. My heart broke when hers did. I was moved to tears as her story unfolded within the pages. I rejoiced and praised God when she overcame the trials and experienced freedom. The Lord, if we let Him, and surrender fully to Him, can truly bring beauty from any mess, no matter how great or small. Sundi Jo is living proof of that.

—Abby Lewis, author, Living Still

Dear Dad chronicles a young woman's journey from despair to hope, as she grieves the loss of her father. Sundi Jo gives the reader a candid look at the raw emotions she experienced during some of her darkest moments. Written as journal entries to her earthly father, she includes her thoughts and prayers to her Heavenly Father, and her longing to be loved. Victory over her past comes in the form of complete surrender to God. While Dear Dad exposes the weaknesses we all face, it paints a beautiful picture of a great God who longs to bring us triumph from tragedy.

—Maria I. Morgan, writer, mariaimorgan.com

Sundi Jo's book Dear Dad is a beautiful story of a trial that God has turned into a triumph. Everyone needs to read a story like this to be encouraged in difficult times, inspired to be a blessing or simply recharge your "spiritual batteries". It is written with love towards the reader and, above all, the passion towards our Creator, the greatest Father for those who follow Him.

—Helen Todd, vice president, World Missions Alliance

In Dear Dad, author Sundi Jo Graham shares more than her own Father/Daughter story with us, her readers. She boldly, yet gently, shares our story. No matter who you are or what kind of experiences you've had, you will see your own reflection within the pages of this book. Princess, you owe it to yourself to breathe in deeply what Sundi Jo offers!

—Shelley Hendrix, author, founder of Church4Chicks

Few people convey their stories with such honesty and detail as Sundi Jo does. Not one to share simply for the sake of storytelling, Sundi Jo tells them in the hope that we, too, can learn from them and possibly avoid the pain she's walked through. Dear Dad is no different. It's a powerful account of the beauty and freedom that are ours through grace.

—Jessica Bufkin, editor, Single Roots

Dear Dad is a must read for anyone who has struggled with control, death, addiction, or relationships. All of us. Sundi Jo's honest retelling of her struggles resonates with readers, giving voice to struggles we have all experienced but don't often acknowledge. Lives are changed through story. And this story will change many.

—Sarah Farish, writer, blogger, teacher

Important relationships are never easy. When your earthly father is distant, awkward, absent, so far from perfect, how hard is it to embrace the idea of God as your heavenly Father? When years of abuse at the hands of those you should trust builds a wall around your heart, how hard is it to tear down and let God – and others – in? Dear Dad is the raw, heartfelt chronicle of such a journey. In sharing her amazing story of redemption and restoration, Sundi Jo invites us to discover our own inner beauty, to see ourselves through the eyes of our loving and perfect Father.

—Larry Hehn, author, blogger, "Christian in the Rough"

Think you have problems? A deadbeat dad? Addictions? Secrets? Are you gay? Depressed? Do you come from a messed up family? If you answer yes to any of these questions, read this book. Don't miss this gripping, guided journey to healing, forgiveness and freedom. Sundi Jo will take you by the hand and lead you through her transformative year in a way that will have you reaching for the tissue box one moment and a pen the next.

—Marilyn Luinstra, children's leader

Brutally honest, compellingly real, Dear Dad speaks to the heart of every little girl hurt through the negligence of the adults in her life and to the need for freedom and healing for the women they become. Sundi Jo holds nothing back as she relates her painful journey from the brink of destruction to the joy of living at peace with herself and the loving Father who walked with her each step of the way.

—Sarah Fotopulous, author, The Sufficiency of Grace

Dear Dad courageously faces the issues of dependency head on. It explores struggles many Christians face, but are afraid to talk about. Sundi Jo's transparency in her journey through sorrow and emotional pain offers hope to those experiencing similar circumstances. Readers can learn about dependency issues and how to relate to someone experiencing addiction.

Sundi Jo's story demonstrates how God is truly the answer to every problem. This book is one I will treasure in my personal library.

—Kim Jones, author, The Case of the Missing Mountain

Dear Dad is a beautiful story of how one girl realizes she is a princess. Sundi Jo shares the events of her life that left her feeling worthless and out of control. Once her weaknesses were exposed, she was free to find redemption -- a new peace from abuse, rape, alcohol, and homosexuality. If you are longing for a peace that surpasses all, this book will help and challenge you to seek it.

—Alene Snodgrass, author, Graffiti: scribbles from different sides of the street

Don't miss this heartfelt story about walking through despair in order to find hope. Sundi Jo shares authentically and beautifully, but it's more than her story, it's a story for so many others. Her bravery will inspire you to be brave, to find hope in your own difficult circumstances.

—Allison Vesterfelt, managing editor, Prodigal Magazine

Dear Dad

Foreword by Dr. Gary Smalley

Dear Dad,
did you know
I was a
Princess?

Sundi Jo Graham

TATE PUBLISHING
AND ENTERPRISES, LLC

Published by Tate Publishing & Enterprises, LLC
127 E. Trade Center Terrace | Mustang, Oklahoma 73064 USA
1.888.361.9473 | www.tatepublishing.com

Tate Publishing is committed to excellence in the publishing industry. The company reflects the philosophy established by the founders, based on Psalm 68:11,
"The Lord gave the word and great was the company of those who published it."

Book design copyright © 2013 by Tate Publishing, LLC. All rights reserved.
Cover design by Diana Bogardus
Cover buld by Lauro Talibong
Interior design by Mary Jean Archival

Published in the United States of America

ISBN: 978-1-62295-371-4
1. Biography & Autobiography / General
2. Biography & Autobiography / Personal Memoirs
13.02.11

To my earthly father, Doug…
one day we'll have our dance.
To my heavenly Father…
for loving me with an everlasting love.

In 2010, Dr. Gary Smalley looked at me and said, "You should write a book." In 2011, on a 5x7 note card, he gave me a list of what I needed to do to write that book, $40 out of his pocket to buy writing supplies, and his blessing to dream big. Thank you Gary for believing in me and pushing me to do the same.

Jennifer, there aren't enough thank-you's in the world to say to you. Your unending grace and mercy in my life has given me a glimpse of what the grace of our Heavenly Father is like. Thank you for walking through this journey with me, and your commitment to loving me through the good and bad.

Jammie, God has proved through you and I that the bonds of friendship are worth fighting for. Thank you for staying by my side through thick and thin.

Thank you Ted Burden for being the one who showed me what loving Jesus was all about. Every hug and smile from you is like Jesus smiling back at me.

Caleb, you brighten up my life and I can't imagine it without you. You have a piece of my heart not many have. I love you more than you'll ever know.

Thank you to my friends and family for encouraging me in the writing of this book. Thank you for the emails, texts, and phone calls to inspire me to keep going.

Thank you to the prayer team that prayed circles around the book months before it ever came to be. This book wouldn't be without you.

Mom, I couldn't have written this book without you. Thank you for dreaming big with me. Thank you for the idea behind the book. Without your input, I couldn't have put the words on the pages. God has grown our relationship beyond what I knew it could be, and for that I'm forever grateful. I love you.

Finally, thank you to my heavenly Father, Jesus Christ. Thank you for pursuing me and calling me by name. I can't wait to spend eternity with you.

Foreword

The first time I met Sundi Jo, I remember seeing the brokenness in her eyes. Though she smiled and made jokes, I knew there was something deeper, a longing for freedom. When I saw her again a few months later, I couldn't believe my eyes! This wasn't the same girl. Her smile was genuine. Her eyes were brighter. She had found the joy she had been longing for.

I remember telling her she should write a book but I never knew she would take me seriously. In 2010 we sat down for lunch and she told me her plans. She wanted me to teach her everything I knew about writing and I was willing. She walked away from our meeting on fire and ready to tell a story that would change lives.

When she told me the name of the title, my eyes welled up with tears immediately. I knew this was a message millions of women, teenagers, little girls, and even men would need to hear. Her willingness to be so real and honest, putting aside her own fears to touch the hearts of others, is inspiring. I can't wait for you to read it.

For the past three years I have watched Sundi Jo go from being defeated to being a conqueror. Her heart is on fire to show others it's never too late to restore your relationships.

This book is for anyone searching for answers, seeking hope in a broken world. And I assure you will laugh along the way. Whether you struggle with fear, pride, shame, or more, watching her story and restoration unfold on these pages will give you hope and change your heart. This is a read that will move you to tears and bring a few laughs along the way.

—Dr. Gary Smalley
Author of *The DNA of Relationships*

August 23, 2009

It's Sunday. I did the deal today. I woke up and went to church. My routine was a little different than most days. No makeup. I'm not sure I even brushed my hair. I found a T-shirt in the hamper. I honestly couldn't tell you if it was clean. I simply didn't care. Still don't. I looked in the mirror this morning, but I couldn't recognize who was staring back at me. They were the eyes of a stranger. I sat by Jammie in the service today. I think we were both trying to pretend like last night was a distant memory. It's more distant for me than her at this point I'm sure. I only remember bits and pieces. Pastor Ted B. asked me if I was okay. Of course I lied and said, "Great." Something tells me he knows I'm completely full of it.

Sundays at Woodland Hills Family Church used to be my favorite day of the week. Wake up early and get ready. Pop my daily dose of oatmeal and raisins in the microwave and head off to the church in the big, purple castle inside a theme park. Being in the media booth used to be fun. Turn the screens on. Find just the right background for the worship songs (there is an art to it really). Set the video camera just right. Get the podcast ready. Standing in the back watching people with their hands in the air worshiping used to bring a smile to my face. Now it's just part of the routine like everything else. I wake up, listen to Joyce Meyer, go to the gym, go to work, lead a small group, go to bed, then get up and do it all over again. None of it has a purpose anymore. Every day is just another day. I keep telling myself that God is in it somewhere, but I can't guess where. We'll see if he shows up; he hasn't so far.

I managed to sleep for an hour this afternoon. That's a big step for me. I can't even tell you what time it is right now. My mind is in another galaxy. I can tell you it's dark outside, and I so desperately want to talk with you. I stare at your picture, but you say nothing. Satan keeps talking to me. I can hear him. He's all over the place. Did you know that was possible? He keeps telling me to drink the wine. I'm tempted. What do you think? I hear his voice dancing around in my head again, wreaking havoc with my thoughts. He tells me to drink it; drink it and you will talk to me.

Do you know I have barely slept in eighteen days? I think I'm losing my mind. People tell me I'm not, but I think I have them fooled. No one seems to understand. I just want someone to see what is going on in my head. I want someone to feel what I'm feeling. I want someone to see the dreams that I see when I close my eyes. They would understand then why I don't sleep. *Understand*, that is such an overused word. What does it mean anyway? In the dreams strangers capture me. They beat me until I'm unrecognizable. They carry me to far away places, rape me, and leave me for dead. No one finds me. No one recognizes me. I'm alone in a desolate place, full of shame with no chance of rescue. Do you understand? Of course you don't, you're dead.

The laughter echoes in this room. Do you think Satan has a red tail, horns, and carries around a pitchfork? Me neither. I can hear him, but I don't see him. Maybe he is too big of a coward to show his face. I have a full bottle of St. James Red Velvet sitting in my hand, and I'm talking to a picture of a dead man. I know the truth. Somewhere in this moment I should be laughing. I think I've forgotten how to do that. Laughter is overrated. The truth is I will never hear your voice again, but I would rather believe the lie. Talk to me! Say something! Don't just stare.

Thoughts of Saturday night's disaster keep running through my head. All we were planning to do was go to the bar and have a drink. Do you ever get that feeling in your gut when you absolutely know without a doubt that you are supposed to be doing something else? We pulled into the parking lot and that feeling hit me. I stayed quiet for a moment and tried to get the feeling to go away. It only got stronger as our footsteps got closer to the front door. As Jammie and I reached Waxy O'Shea's Irish Pub, my heart stopped. I was just there last week with a friend, and I didn't have that feeling. This was different. I could barely catch my breath. Tears trickled down my cheek. Jammie looked at me with an odd look.

"Let's just go home," I told her. We didn't.

I sat down at the bar and waited. Maybe the bartender wouldn't notice me. Maybe I could disappear into the crowd like a wallflower. I wanted to bolt toward the front door, but I didn't.

"What can I get for you?" he asked.

Do you think he's ever seen someone order a drink with a teardrop strolling down her face?

"I'll have a Bud Light."

"Bottle or draft?"

My mind raced. *Do I really have to decide how I want to drink it? Just give me a beer!* It wasn't too late to go home. We could turn around and go right now. I'm sure he thought I was nuts. Oh, if he only knew. The next thing I remember is the burning sensation of tequila as it tickled my throat. The smell and the taste turned my stomach. I'm sure the look on my face didn't hide the disgust either.

As if I hadn't done enough to make a fool of myself, the night only got better. As Janie Pruitt made her way toward me, I tried to hide my face. How pathetic was it that I, her small group leader, the one who proclaimed Jesus Christ on Tuesday night, was sitting drunk at the bar on Saturday night? What a hypocrite! I would love to remember what I said to her, but I don't. Then again, maybe it's best I don't know. Jammie drove me home.

She tells me I just kept crying and telling her I just wanted her to understand, but again, I don't remember. Maybe that's best. It's hard to apologize for things you don't remember. If she didn't understand me last night, she certainly won't tonight. The last thing I recall is watching her walk out the door as I sat on my couch in a pool of pathetic tears. What are the tears good for anyway? They make me weak, and I cannot afford to be weak. I don't want emotion. I don't want laughter. I want nothing. I want to feel absolutely nothing. Emptiness. Is this what the life of an alcoholic looks like? Is that what you wanted? Did you want to be nothing? Did you enjoy the emptiness? Let's get one thing straight. You are the alcoholic, not me!

My eyes feel heavy. Maybe that's a sign I can get some sleep. I snuggle up on the cozy, red couch, sticking my finger in the hole of the pillow that Skeeter had for a snack. At least I have Skeeter. She's the only one that gets me. She knows everything, and she still sticks around. That's the loyalty of a dog for you.

Today I have let myself reach a completely new level of despair. I feel it all coming to an end.

August 24, 2009

I managed to sleep for a couple hours last night. I didn't give myself enough time for the dreams to control me. I attempted to talk with God, but I didn't have much to say. What is there to say? What do you talk about with someone who doesn't seem to answer you back?

You want to hear a funny story? I had a meeting with my boss today. I managed to keep myself alert enough to pretend I was listening to him. I did manage to hear "doing a great job," "setting a great example for the others," and "great work." He's so full of crap, and he doesn't even realize it. What example do I set? I'm a freak pretending to be normal. Maybe I should have told him I was going on day nineteen of completely losing every ounce of sanity.

Jennifer told me today I needed to get back on my medication. She's only been my friend for a year, yet it seems she's known me all of my life. Sometimes I love that, other times I hate it. The doctor put me on Buspar last September to help with my anxiety. I decided in April I didn't want to take it anymore. It wasn't helping; they just made things worse. I didn't want to be like you, depending on a pill for everything. I'll admit it might not have been the smartest thing. Of course I won't admit that to anyone but you.

"It's time to get back on some medication from the doctor—like the stuff you took yourself off of. Your sleeping problems are making this situation worse—making you more tired and depressed and clouding your judgment."

If she only knew. She keeps trying to get me to talk to her. Do I tell her what she wants to hear or tell the truth? What is the truth?

I tried so hard to be normal today. I managed to make it through the whole day, but the voices in my head never went away. I waited for odd looks from my coworkers, but nothing. I went to the bathroom and talked to the voices so people wouldn't catch on. Maybe I am normal and the rest of the world is crazy.

I tried to talk to God today. I don't know how well that worked, but I tried.

I sit here today, and I feel numb. I'm trying to understand how I feel, but I don't know. Is it because I refuse to want to know? Is it because I refuse to let myself think about it? How did I get where I am right now? Three weeks ago I was full of faith, praising you. Last night I let myself get drunk, again. After the way I felt when I woke up yesterday morning, I had no desire to drink. Then last night, here I sat with a bottle of wine in my hand.

Who am I becoming? How does this happen? How does it happen so fast?

I'm so ashamed of who I'm allowing myself to become. But if I'm so ashamed, why do I continue to let it happen? I feel like I'm losing all my strength. I'm sabotaging everything in my life. Everything! I'm so tired. My body is so tired. My mind is so tired. I feel like I just need a day—a day to just sleep.

Why do I want to destroy every good thing that happens to me? People have got to think I'm crazy. I can be okay one minute and not the next. How is that possible? God, please don't give up on me. I'm so sorry. I'm sorry I'm hurting you. Please don't give up on me.

Why did you take Caleb? I want him to come home! I'm sorry for whatever I've done to send him away, but please bring him back. I'm lost without him here. I trust you in knowing that you will keep him safe. I've kept pretty silent about it since he left in May, but I can't take the heartbreak anymore. He's not even my child, but I feel so lost without him. I want his pictures off my wall! I don't want to look at him anymore. I just want to forget, and then I won't hurt.

Right now, this very moment, I just want you take me. I don't want to live anymore! I don't want to hurt anymore. I feel so lost. I don't deserve any good thing you give me. None of it! I'm drying my tears right now. I will cry no more!

I feel so lost. I look up verses, I try to read your word, and my mind is so busy that I can't read it. I zoom through it so fast. By the time I get to the end, I've lost my attention. I can't concentrate. I want to, but my mind won't stop running. I can't be still. I want to.

I have no one to take care of. I'm alone. I feel alone. Everyone is gone. What am I supposed to do? I'm afraid to be alone.

Jennifer says there's a little girl inside of me that needs to be taken care of. Where is she? I feel like that little girl is dead; she never existed. I stopped being a little girl when I was mixing my dad's drink at six years old. I stopped being a little girl when I watched him hit my mom and step-mom. I stopped when my mom wasn't around to be my mom. I stopped in the third grade when Mrs. Baker let me know how worthless I was. I stopped being a little girl the first time I was molested. I've never been a little girl.

I want to find you. I need help.

I can't stand this apartment! It's so dark in here. I can see smog all around me. You know the dew that rises on the lake in the morning? It seems beautiful from afar until you get right up to it, and then you can't breathe. The thickness surrounds you, and the heaviness rests on your shoulders. I'm sitting in that.

All I wanted to do today was come home and sleep, but when I walked in the door and saw the fog, I lost it. Maybe you would talk to me this time. Maybe I could try again. I pulled into the gas station and sat with the car running for what seemed like eternity. I could feel something tugging at me. *Just turn around and go home. No one will know.* Was that God talking to me now? He was a little late. As I walked back to the wine department, I got a text message from Jennifer. It was John 4:13-14. *Jesus answered, "Everyone who drinks this water will be thirsty again, but whoever drinks the water I give him will never thirst. Indeed, the water I give him will become in him a spring of water welling up to eternal life."* How did she know? Was it God? He was finally reaching out. Now what? I could have put it up, turned around, and went home, and no one would have known, but I didn't. As I walked up to the counter to pay, she sent another text. Ecclesiastes 2:3 flashed across the screen, *"The king tried everything, including intoxicating drink, to see if it satisfied. It did not."* What was I to do with that? He is enough to satisfy. Even kings cannot be satisfied. Was I doing it for satisfaction? Had I tried everything? I certainly wasn't doing it because I was thirsty. It was too late. I couldn't turn around now; I would embarrass myself.

I made a list at work today of reasons I wouldn't drink tonight:

- I'll gain weight.
- I'm hurting those around me.
- I'm hurting God.
- I'm letting the devil win.
- I can't make good decisions when drinking.
- I have the possibility of becoming an addict like the rest of my family.
- It's not who I am.
- I don't need to cover up my problems; I need to deal with them.

Of course the weight gain would be my first concern. I haven't lost ninety pounds for nothing.

So, here it is, 8:00 p.m., and the wine is gone. How does a person get drunk on a bottle of wine? I guess without sleep it adds to the effect. I sat outside tonight talking to the man in the moon. Of course he didn't talk back. Well, I guess the secret is over. I think Jennifer is on to me after our unusual Gmail chat conversation.

"I see the man in the moon," I said.

"What does he look like?"

"He wears overalls, flip flops, a ball cap, has blonde hair, and beautiful eyes. He hangs there and watches the world. Do you think he ever gets lonely?"

"He sounds like Toby Keith."

"He looks more innocent than Toby Keith."

She laughed. "What are you doing?"

"Sitting on my deck watching the man in the moon."

"Very nice."

"Yeah, he hasn't talked to me yet, though. It reminds me of the Conway Twitty song. 'He said I can move oceans when I take the notion. Or make mountains tremble and rivers run dry. But in all matters human, remember there's someone in charge of those things way above you and I.'"

"Are you sober? Drinking?" I avoided the question.

Then the phone rang. It was Caleb. How could I screw this up? Every night I'm supposed to read him the Bible and tuck him into bed over the phone. I had to answer the phone.

"Crap!"

"What?" Jennifer asked.

"I have to sober up. I have to! Caleb is on the phone, and I have to read the Bible. I can't do this. Oh, I screwed up big time." I closed the laptop.

For a few moments I managed the "act" of being normal. I read our daily verses from the book of Romans, prayed with him, and then we hung up.

I sat back on the couch, watching the wine bottle spin on the coffee table. How did I let this happen? How did I get this far? All I wanted to do was keep the dreams from happening. All I want to do is understand. I just want it to all go away.

I opened the laptop again and entered the Google world. There it was: all the pornography I could get my hands on. I had over 95,000 pornography sites at my fingertips within seconds. Maybe that would soothe the emptiness inside of me. Maybe that would fill the void. It had been three years since I allowed myself to go down that deep tunnel of darkness. It was 2006. I remember the day like it was yesterday. I felt completely alone, like everyone had left again. I was filled with shame and secrets. I still hold the secrets in my heart. I promised God and myself that I would never do it again. But there I was. I was disgusted with myself. I picked up the laptop, threw it, and cried myself to sleep, once again begging God to forgive me.

Tomorrow would be better. Tomorrow I would be normal again. Tomorrow.

August 25, 2009

I called Caleb and prayed he wouldn't answer. I didn't want him to hear the crackling in my voice from the hundreds of tears I cried this morning. He didn't answer. I left a message. "Hi, buddy. Just want to say that I love you and I will talk to you soon." I had just lied to the little boy through voicemail. I had no idea when I would hear his voice again. Will I ever hear his voice again? Though we're just cousins, he and I have a relationship that has been through so much. I can't imagine my life without him. We turned into the rocky driveway, down a forest-covered path that felt like the jungle swooping in on me. I held my breath, and tears streamed down my face. Jammie grabbed my hand from the backseat. Jennifer grabbed my other hand as she guided us down the path. She was singing in a whisper, "I need you, Jesus, to come to my rescue. Where else can I go?" I was comforted for a tiny moment.

Then we pulled into the driveway of the Table Rock Freedom Center. I grasped onto their hands tighter, as my heart beat faster and faster. As Jennifer began to pray, I was startled by a knock on the window and a burst of laughter and excitement from Fran Mead, director of TRFC. Her face lit up with a big smile. She was excited enough for the both of us because I certainly did not feel the same. I stepped out of the car with a tiny suitcase behind me that Jammie had packed.

We all sat in Fran's office as my palms got sweaty and my knees got weak. None of this could be real. I was just here a month ago celebrating the Fourth of July with the women who lived here. How is it possible that this is now my home? I hugged Fran every Sunday morning at church. I am a volunteer here, not a resident.

The Table Rock Freedom Center is a residential, Christ-centered recovery program for women with life-controlling issues. So what? I can control everything just fine. I just need some time to get things in order.

"So what's going on?" asked Fran as she looked at me. I couldn't speak.

"She's been having some serious nightmares for several months, and now she hasn't been sleeping. She's been drinking for the last four days," said Jennifer as she took a glance at me, then a glimpse back at Fran.

"We can definitely help," Fran said. "The girls would love to have you here, and so would I."

Everyone was smiling except me. And when I heard the words *twelve months*, there was no remote chance of a smile. I flashed back to the two hours before. I was lied to. I knew it!

"You'll be done in no time, Sundi Jo," Jennifer said.

"No I won't! It's like a year."

She wouldn't listen. These people expect me to stay here for a year. For what? Because I have nightmares? Because I drank some wine? I can't have my phone. I can't have my laptop. They don't even watch television here. This is crazy!

"I knew this would happen. I knew I was going to be here," I said in a whisper.

"What do you mean?" Jennifer asked.

"I've been having a recurring dream. Each time I see the words *Table Rock Freedom Center* in bright lights on a neon sign. This all makes sense."

That dream came true as tonight I'm lying in a twin-sized bed in a strange place. Everyone sleeps as I stare at the ceiling. I'm not even covered up with my own blanket. My dog isn't next to me. I've never felt so alone! Where is my home? Flashbacks of the day fill my mind.

I went to the gym early this morning. Sleep last night was very minimal, so I decided I might as well get up and go. Then I met Jennifer for coffee at Panera Bread before going to work. I was bound and determined to be functional today. I walked in and there she sat in a cozy, quiet corner just waiting. I knew then this wasn't going to be a typical coffee conversation.

We had small talk for a few minutes, as she asked me about my plans for the weekend. Then she got to the point.

"What's going on with you?"

"Nothing," I said as I held my head low and looked the other way. Making eye contact was not on my agenda.

"You're lying."

"I'm fine!"

She leaned forward, clasped her hands together between her knees, and closed her eyes. I'm guessing she was asking God what to say. She opened her eyes, and I briefly caught a glimpse of the sadness in her eyes before I looked back down at the floor.

"I'm worried about you," she said with desperation in her voice. "I just want to snuggle up with you and hold you while you cry. I want you to be okay."

"Just leave me alone. I will be fine!"

"You're not fine, and we both know that."

"You can't tell my mom about any of this. You know she will not make this better."

"Well, that all depends on what you do. That depends on what you're willing to do."

"I just want to cry and I can't," I said as I stared at the high-top table in front of me.

She put her hand on my knee and said, "I want to help you. Let's go to the car and cry. I'll take you home and you can cry." The sadness in her voice was breaking me. I so desperately wanted to push her away, but I couldn't anymore.

There was silence. I could feel my body giving in. I could feel my emotions giving way. I could feel it was all coming to an end.

"I'm so tired. I just want to die."

She threw her hands in the air and said, "Okay, that's it. You're either going coming to work with me or I'm following you to work."

The conversation had just gone in a completely different direction.

"I'm an adult. I don't need you to babysit me!"

"You just told me you wanted to die. I'm not letting you go by yourself," she said sternly. I was too tired to fight with her. Giving in was my only option at that point.

As I drove to work with Jennifer directly behind me, I got angrier at each turn. I was being followed like a little child. I pulled into the parking lot at 9:00 a.m., slammed the car door shut, and walked into the office for another day. I was safely at work, and my babysitter could now stop worrying about me.

Ten minutes later I walked back outside to see Jennifer was still sitting in the parking lot. I stormed through the front doors and to her car.

"Why are you still here?" "You need to leave!"

"I'll leave when it's time."

"This is bull," I said, as I stomped back through the parking lot.

When I looked back out the window five minutes later, there was Ted B. I immediately felt the heat rise in my body. This couldn't be happening. I couldn't talk. I was too mad.

"Why are you doing this?" I asked her via text message. "Just leave!"

Then they were gone. I wanted this to all be over. I sat at my desk twirling a pencil around, trying to figure out how to make sense of everything. No one else was in the office yet. I was extremely grateful. I was going to talk to Jammie. Maybe she would help me make sense of everything. Then I saw her e-mail:

"I was reading this morning and came across these scriptures and wanted to share it with you:

"Is anyone among you sick? Let him call for the elders of the church, and let them pray over him, anointing him with oil in the name of the Lord. And the prayer of faith will save the sick, and the Lord will raise him up" James 5:14-15.

"For I will restore health to you and heal you of your wounds, says the Lord" Jeremiah 30:17.

"Bless the Lord, O my soul, and forget not all His benefits: who forgives all your iniquities, who heals all your diseases" Psalm 103:2-3.

"I love you and hope that you can meditate on these, and maybe they will help you want to seek help from our church family."

Seek help from our church family? I had no idea what she was talking about. They had dragged her into all of this, too.

"Hi," I typed to her in an instant message.

"Hi."

"This is getting blown so out of proportion."

"What?"

"All of this. I will be fine. I just need some time."

"Are you referring to my e-mail? I just thought that might be something to help you."

"No, I'm not referring to your e-mail. Thank you for the verses. I appreciate them."

"Well, if you are referring to breakfast, Sundi Jo, your friends are just concerned about you. And with drinking, you of all people know that the longer it goes on the worse it gets. The harder the chain is to break. So more time with that is not the answer. More time to heal…that is understandable. My grandma has been gone for almost two years, and I'm still not over it. But you of all people told me I have to go on."

"I know that. This is ridiculous! You guys act like I've been drinking for six months. I am so pissed off right now!"

"Why?"

"Nothing. Never mind."

"Love you very much, Jilly Jo Marie."

"That's what everybody keeps saying, as they do all this crap behind my back. You need to explain to Jen that Mom can't find out about this. You know, Jammie, that she wouldn't help the situation. She would only make it worse.

"I will talk to her."

I had meetings to concentrate on today. I had a proposal that was due yesterday. I had a presentation to tweak that I had been working on for two weeks. I couldn't even remember how to answer the phone. I prayed silently that it wouldn't ring. It didn't. This was all going to go away. It didn't.

I made an attempt to talk to Jennifer.

"I so don't want to be here," I typed in an instant message. "I can't freaking concentrate."

"I am so sorry," she typed back.

"Can we please just pretend this isn't happening? Please just make this whole day go away."

"No."

"This isn't fair, Jen!"

"What would make this fair, SJ?"

"You guys are backing me into a corner. You're making it more than it is."

"I don't see it that way at all. When would be the appropriate time to intervene from your perspective? How long would you wait for me before you did something?"

"Never mind. I shouldn't have even brought it up." I knew I was not winning this argument.

"I just need to go home and get some sleep."

"I am sorry you are so tired."

"No big deal."

"Yes it is. It makes me very sad for you, and exhaustion makes a big difference in a person's ability to cope. Working so hard to make sure everything looks and seems okay is a lot of work and can only last so long. It wears a person out. I know this from experience."

She knew what? She knew what being crazy felt like? She knew what being backed into a corner felt like? I wanted to be so mad at her.

"Okay. I would never hurt your heart on purpose. I don't want to hurt you," I typed.

"I know you don't."

As people started to make their way into the office, I pushed back the events of the morning so that I could seem normal, if only for a moment. Someone else was there to answer the phone. I could sit in my back corner office and get some work done. I wanted to anyway. Until, that was, I received a text message from Jennifer asking to meet with her and Ted B. in the afternoon. Fear immediately took over. What could they possibly want? Why would my pastor need to talk to me? What did she tell him? Why is she talking to other people about me? This was all a mess.

I was back in the corner. Here were my friends and my pastor wanting a meeting. It was real. It was becoming real. My secret was out. I wanted to run. Where would I go? Where could I go? A wave of relief took over me when I learned my boss wouldn't be back in the office until later that afternoon, so I couldn't meet at the appointed time. But, they were willing to reschedule. How generous of them. Regardless, I wasn't functioning at work and decided to go home early. I told my boss I wasn't feeling well and planned to go home at 1:30 p.m. I was being asked to pick a time that was convenient for me for our meeting. There was no time of convenience.

"I'm going home," I instant messaged to Jennifer.

"To do what? Sleep?"

"No, to count the dots on the ceiling," I sarcastically typed back. "I'm sorry, I take that back."

"Okay—Ted, Jammie, and I love you and want to help you. We have a great solution for your situation and want to discuss it with you today. Our desire is that you would listen to us. We will not force you to do anything. Call me or Jammie and give us a time that you will meet us."

I walked out the doors of the office at 1:30 p.m., wondering if I would ever see the place again. I was on my way home to get some sleep, silently hoping I wouldn't wake up. On my way I stopped trying to keep the tears back. I let them go. I screamed at God, "Why are you doing this? Please tell them just to leave me alone!"

I pulled into the parking lot of the convenience store and walked straight back to the liquor department with puffy cheeks and red eyes. I picked up two twenty-four-ounce cans of Natural Light and threw my money on the counter as the clerk put them into brown paper bags. This was my first "brown bag special."

I immediately felt like you. I was you. I was becoming you. I am you. I sat in the car with a brown bag next to me and your fury taking over me. I walked into my apartment. Someone had been in there. My wine bottles were gone. The trash had been taken out. I knew it had to be Jammie. I called and asked her why she was in my apartment.

"I just wanted to make sure you didn't have anything else in there," she said.

"It's none of your business!" I harshly stated before hanging up.

I sat on my couch and drank the first beer. Then I opened the second one. I stared at it. Watching it sweat through the bag, I could smell the stench of it as it soaked into my shirt from spilling it. I couldn't do this anymore.

I picked up the phone and dialed Jennifer. She answered immediately.

"Sundi Jo, are you okay?"

I sat in silence as I tried to contain the flood of tears that had just started.

"I need help," I said in a slurred whisper, "I need help."

"I'll be right there, okay? Don't do anything. I'll be there."

I picked up the beer and held it in my hands. I was you sitting on the couch. I was at the bottom. I had done what I always swore I would never do. I became you. A few minutes later, Jammie walked in the door. She walked over and tried to take the beer out of my hand. I pulled away with a smile and wouldn't let her. I couldn't figure out why I was smiling. Maybe if I laughed it would all be over. I hated you at that moment. Hated you because I was so much like you. But if I let go would there be anything left of you?

"Why are you smiling?" she asked.

"Why are you here?" I asked back.

She didn't say anything. I laid my head back against the couch with a grip on the beer can. Then Jennifer walked through the door. The door didn't close. There was someone else. Angela Jennings, the youth director of Woodland Hills Family Church, was behind her. This was being turned into an event. I couldn't care. I was too weak to care. Jennifer grabbed the beer from my hand, and I didn't fight it anymore. She sat on the edge of the couch and put her hand on my shoulder.

"It's going to be okay."

I nodded in agreement, until I saw Ted B.'s Jeep pull into the driveway. I looked at Jammie and Jennifer. I was completely being set up. I reluctantly agreed to meet Ted outside. I walked down the steps of my apartment with a beer stain on my T-shirt, mascara smeared down my cheeks, broken sunglasses, and the smell of alcohol on my breath to meet my pastor. I couldn't look him in the eyes. I sat on the bottom step as he walked toward me.

"Listen," he said, "I'm not your dad. I'm not your grandpa. But I'm going to talk to you like you were my own daughter. You need help. There is a bed open for you at the Table Rock Freedom Center. They are willing to help you. You need ten days worth of clothes, and we will get the rest later."

"Are you freaking serious?" I started to defend myself before he quickly interrupted.

"You need help, SJ. You know that. We all want to help you. We will take care of everything for you. You just have to be willing to get help."

"I have to pee."

I walked back upstairs and headed straight for the bathroom. I leaned up against the wall next to the bathtub, straight across from the toilet and melted into the floor. I leaned my head against the edge of the bathtub and sobbed. I knew it wouldn't be long before the rest followed, and sure enough, there they were, four women in a tiny bathroom. Jennifer sat on the toilet, Angela on the floor, and Jammie stood in the hallway.

"Why are you doing this?" I cried through desperate tears. "Please make this go away! I just need some time! I just need time!"

"Sundi Jo, we are just trying to help you," Jennifer said. "This is a chance for you to get some help. They will help you with your nightmares. They will help you grieve your dad's death. They will help you."

"What am I going to do with my apartment? What about my job? What about my dog?"

"You will find another job," said Jammie. "You can't work there right now the way you are anyway."

"We'll take care of your apartment, and Jammie and I both can take care of Skeeter," Jennifer said.

Angela chimed in, "I know you don't want to be like your dad. This is your chance to get help." How did she know that? How did she know I felt exactly like you?

After about two hours, realizing I was fighting a losing game and after Jammie had packed my suitcase, I walked down the steps to Ted B. waiting patiently in the August heat.

"You're going to be happy you made this decision," he said. He hugged me. Then he was gone.

As I walked past my car toward Jennifer's, I looked in the backseat and saw my Bible. It had been lying there for two weeks. I hadn't opened it. I hadn't acknowledged it. Maybe that was my first mistake.

I watched Jammie and Jennifer walk out the door tonight. Just like that it seemed they were gone. I sat down at the dining room table in my beer-stained blouse for a dinner of spaghetti I could barely touch. Janet Perkins sat next to me and grabbed my hand. "It will be okay. You're doing the right thing." How humbling was this? I was Janet's small group leader. We were supposed to be sitting around my living room at this time doing a Bible study. Instead she was serving me dinner around a table of three other women. For a split second I wanted to smile at God's sense of humor.

Everything comfortable is gone. Everyone is gone. Am I that bad? Did I do something that wrong for them to leave? Will I see them again? Will I see anyone again? In an instant my life is different.

God, where are you? What is happening? I'm sorry. I'm sorry for whatever I have done. Please forgive me. Please fix me. Please make this all go away. Don't leave me! I need you now more than ever!

There is still time to get a few hours of sleep. Today is a dream. Tomorrow will be new again.

September 5, 2009

Happy birthday to me! Oh, how I will remember this birthday. I received cards, flowers, and cupcakes; sugar free of course. I have been so humbled over these past two weeks. Tonight I served food and cake at a wedding. On my birthday! There is no sugar or caffeine allowed here. So what did we do? We served punch and a sugar-filled cake. Janet allowed us to each have a piece. I prefer to say that I ate a big chunk of humble cake.

I keep daydreaming about the plans I was supposed to have today. I was supposed to be at the comedy club and having dinner with friends. Instead, I will be in bed by 9:00 p.m. tonight so that I can rise and shine at 5:20 in the morning to serve coffee at church. Do I sound a little bitter? I am. The girls tell me the sooner I stop fighting and give into my being here it will get easier. Who asked them?

Fran tells me I have to be willing to ask for help. I don't need help. Why would I trust these girls to help me? They don't even know me. Why would I trust Fran to help me? Her job is to sit in a chair, tell me what's wrong with me, and bring home a paycheck. She can do her work, I'll do my thing, and we'll get this over with in eleven more months.

Jesus, I don't want to be this way. I don't want to be angry. I want to understand. Help me to understand. Just get me through this.

September 12, 2009

I'm sad that I don't feel safe with the girls in the house. I wish they weren't jealous of me. I wish they could be happy for my success. Instead, they talk behind my back as if I don't know. They gripe and complain about things I do but don't have the guts enough to say it to my face. Jennifer said I would be safe here. Yeah right!

This place is a joke. It's a freaking circus. People run around pretending they like you and then stab you in the back the minute you turn around. Sure, I'm insecure, too. We've all got our issues. There's nothing I hate more, though, than someone pretending to be your friend when they're full of crap. Remind me how this is better than being in the world. I could do this in the real world.

September 14, 2009

Lauren and I talked for a while this morning. I told her about the jealousy issues. She said I avoid things too much. I agree that's something I should work on. Why wouldn't I avoid things? Who can I trust to be real with?

This afternoon, things got heated between Tori and me. She admitted she was jealous of me and started to blow her top. She got some things off her chest about me moving so fast in my growth. "I waited too long to change, and when I see you growing so much it makes me jealous and mad at myself," she said. By the time it was over, she was proud of me, we were both crying, and things were better.

September 21, 2009

I woke up this morning to this verse: Isaiah 47:10, *"You have trusted in your wickedness and have said, 'No one sees me.' Your wisdom and knowledge mislead you when you say to yourself, 'I am, and there is none besides me.'"*

I find myself wondering why I counted on myself and not God. I got scared and stopped trusting him.

After I cried out to you and still had the dreams, I didn't know what to do. I'm sorry that I left you. I don't want to handle things on my own anymore. Too many times I have trusted in my own wickedness. Too many times I have gotten caught up in my own desires and my own sin that I thought I was the only one who could see me. Forgive me.

Fran pulled me into the RV today for my session. The fact that I'm getting therapy in a travel trailer makes me laugh. We are in Illinois for the next eight days staying with the most amazing God-loving couple. It is our goal to talk about TRFC to several churches and raise awareness. It's at least nice to have a change of scenery for a little bit. I thought of you today as I stepped inside the RV. Actually, I thought of you, then of calling Jeff Foxworthy. You might be a redneck if...you have your session in an RV.

Fran asked me today if I was being real or not. She wants to know if I trust her. I guess I do. I want to. I'm more than willing to open up and talk, but I don't know what to say. I don't know where I am supposed to start. I told her bits and pieces about my childhood and how I practically raised myself. You were never around, and Mom was always working. She says that explains why I am so codependent and why I have a hard time asking for help.

"It's your time to receive and not give," Fran said.

October 11, 2009

I've been here almost two months. Yesterday I was done. Today I feel peace. How does it all happen so quickly? I write this today with a calmness I haven't felt in years. There is lightness in my step I have never recognized before.

Yesterday my thoughts and emotions were out of control. One minute I was numb, feeling nothing. The next I felt as though my breaking heart was going to leap out of my chest. Why did I hurt so badly? Why wouldn't God hear my cries? I wanted to leave. I wanted to run. But I couldn't. I begged God to let me go home. Every time I would ask, I could hear him say, "Surrender." I didn't want to stay. I didn't belong here.

We had our group session yesterday. I sat in silence as Tori, Lauren, and Katie stared expectantly waiting for me to talk about my issues. My issues were none of their business. I finally gave in.

How do you tell someone what you need when you don't know what you need? What did I feel? I was angry. I was angry with God. I was scared. Every lie in my mind told me I had been abandoned. You were gone. Caleb was gone. Jammie and Jennifer were gone. I had been left, like I always knew I would be once I trusted someone. God wasn't there. I kept asking myself why I was so bad.

I had my weekly session. I tried to speak but didn't know what to say. I was scared. I wanted to run. I couldn't wrap my mind around things. I started to ask myself, *Do I run when things get hard?* Then the truth started to come.

Two days before, I had fasted and prayed. I made my plans. I was ready to go home. I asked God, "What do you want me to do?" He said, "Stay." But my mind played out my going home. I craved it. I craved talking to Caleb every day. I craved freedom. "I am not free here, God. Let me go home, and I'll show you how well I can do. Just let me go home." I begged and pleaded with him. I sat down to work on my Bible study,

Preparing to Hear From God, and day one was titled "Simple Obedience."

"Don't do this to me, God. Let me be obedient at home, please. Please don't punish me."

The word *surrender* hit my heart. I pushed it away. I read the Bible, looking for answers to please me. Every scripture pointed to obedience. Why? Why is this happening to me? I heard the song "Rescue Me" again that night, and it took me back to the first day as we pulled into the driveway. It was another reminder that I couldn't leave. I hated it.

"Have you surrendered to him, honey?" asked Fran, the program director.

I held my breath. How did she know that? How did she know he had told me that time and time again? I could only hold my breath so long before the sobs started. I wish you could have experienced what it was like having God call upon you. Maybe you did. I hope you did.

I kept hearing the words *come to me.* I grasped onto my shirt. The room was silent. I could hear Fran breathing. Then I heard, "I want you." I grabbed my shirt so tight I thought I had ripped it. Someone was pulling on me. I tried harder and harder to stay seated on the couch. The tugging got stronger. I fought it until I couldn't fight anymore. All of a sudden my knees hit the floor and I sobbed. I cried out, "He wants me, Fran! He wants me!"

"Surrender to him, honey. Surrender to him!"

"I don't know how! I want to! I want to so bad!"

She got on her knees beside me and held onto my arm.

"Give it to him. Give it all to him," she whispered.

"I want to! I want to! I'm scared!"

"God has not given you a spirit of fear!"

At that moment I knew it was no longer the two of us in that room. He was there. And I was done! I was done living for myself. The words poured out from the deepest parts of my being.

"Take it, God! Take all of me! Take every ounce of me. I want You to have it all. From the top of my head to the bottom of my toes, Lord, I give it all to you. Fill me up. Fill up every ounce of my being. I don't want to live for me anymore. I want to live for you. I don't want to be scared anymore. I don't want mediocre anymore. I don't want the natural anymore. I want the supernatural! I want you. I want you! I want you!"

Then the words came, "I surrender! I surrender!" I lie in that floor with my face to the ground and gave it *all* to him. I repeated the name of Jesus over and over again. We said, "Amen."

The tears were gone. I leaned up against the couch, and Fran leaned up against the chair. I took a breath. I felt what it must feel like for a baby the first time it comes out of its mother's womb and takes its first breath. I felt like I had just taken my first breath—fresh and new. My whole body was just there, existing. My fingertips to my toenails felt different. I couldn't speak. I stared into Fran's eyes, and she stared into mine. It seemed like we were in that spot for hours.

There were no words to be said. The Holy Spirit filled that room. That peace that transcends all understanding was in me. It filled me up. At 8:30 p.m. I walked out of that room feeling higher than I had ever felt before.

Tori, one of my roommates sat on my bed, held my hand, and prayed with me. I grabbed by Bible, put my head on the pillow, and fell asleep with Jesus's name on my lips.

Hours earlier—days earlier—I had been on the most beautiful dance floor. Marble floors. Rose pedals surrounding me. Ice sculptures. There were amazing fountains of water. My gown was gorgeous, my hair like nothing I had ever seen before. Romance filled the air. We danced to the most beautiful music. He swirled me around and whispered sweet nothings into my ear. He held me so securely as he tipped me backward. I closed my eyes and prepared for his lips to touch mine. It was going to be an amazing kiss.

Then I opened my eyes. I was fooled. I had just waltzed with the devil himself. But before I let him kiss me goodnight, my knight in shining armor, Jesus, came to my rescue. Not only did I let him whisk me away, but I also surrendered.

I am done just surviving. I want to live.

Who knew how much one could be controlled by fear? It takes me back to the first week of being here. The night after my arrival, I sat in the bathroom. I quickly learned it was the only place to have peace and quiet in a house full of women. I was crying and asking God why I was here. I remember his gentle whisper in my ear saying, "I have not given you a spirit of fear, but of power, of love, and a sound mind."

That was probably the most played verse in my head. I had heard it a million times from Jennifer. Every time I would have a panic attack, or admit I was scared of something, she would shoot back with that verse.

My third day here a complete stranger walked up to me in a Thursday night chapel service and said, "God told me to tell you he hasn't given you a spirit of fear." Seriously? The lady didn't know me from Adam.

I finally got it on Sunday night at a church service. The Sunday evening service at Skyline Baptist Church was showing the movie *The Sin Eater*. Of course, just when I thought it couldn't get any better, the verse popped up on screen. I finally got it. I think God was telling me to stop being scared.

November 5, 2009

I learned tonight that I have resisted my fears and feelings for so long that it's become a highway. I got some great advice tonight. Someone told me to take the road less traveled. It is time to make my own dirt road.

Show me, Father, how to take your hand. I know you are inviting me to release my fears, thoughts, and feelings. But how do I do that?

You know, I've gone so long telling myself that I didn't have feelings—that I don't know how to express them. Did you know how? What were you afraid of? Were you afraid to let people love you? I do have to say thank you that you were never afraid to tell me how much you loved me. I think you were always too afraid to show me, but you were never afraid to tell me. That says something about our relationship doesn't it?

December 11, 2009

I'm wearing your shirt tonight. My daddy's shirt! I didn't even remember I had it. I took a two-hour pass tonight to celebrate Jammie's birthday with her at dinner. We stopped by my apartment before she brought me back. I saw your fishing pole in the corner. I saw your picture on my entertainment center. There sat the purple velvet case with your ashes in it.

I walked into the bedroom, and there in my closet was your brown New Orleans Saints T-shirt. I sat on my bed and held it as close to me as I could get it. All the burn holes from you falling asleep with a cigarette hanging out of your mouth made me smile. It was the first time I would have given anything to be able to yell at you again for smoking in bed.

That shirt is all I have left of you really. I have a poster board full of pictures from your funeral in the closet, some marbles you collected, and this grungy, old T-shirt.

I feel bad for Jammie. Tonight was supposed to be a celebration, and instead she wound up sitting next to me on the bed, wiping away my crocodile tears as I buried my face into your shirt.

Tonight, again, I don't understand how all of this happened. You were here and then you weren't. I looked around in an apartment that was my home four months ago, and now it's not. My car sits empty outside. I didn't want to come back tonight. I didn't want to come back to this place! But here I am, back in my twin-sized bed, wearing your shirt, staring at your picture, and getting ready for another day tomorrow.

December 14, 2009

So God used me to bring one of the girls to Christ today. Why he chose me I don't know. I woke up this morning with the urge that I needed to talk with her. To be honest, it was the last thing I wanted to do. Long story short, she gave her life to Christ and wants to be baptized. I know this is something I should be more excited about, but it's honestly the last thing on my mind.

I'm so sick of everything! I'm sick of me. I'm sick of this place. I'm sick of everyone pretending like they give a crap about me. I don't know what's wrong with me. Why should I trust anyone? Why should I trust Fran? Why should I trust Jammie? Why should I trust Jennifer? I feel the pressure building up inside of me. The top is about to explode.

Jennifer tells me I need to grieve being here. I'm sick of people telling me what they think I should do. I would like to see her do it. She wouldn't last a day. If one more person tells me I'm feeling sorry for myself, I'm going to lose it!

I have so many things I want to say to her. Why did she make me come here? Was she that sick of me? Was this an easy way to get rid of me? Everyone waited until the day I came here to tell me they were worried about me. She had to go and get everyone else involved. She lied to me! I told her sitting in that bathroom floor that this place was a year. No one would listen to me.

She just wanted me to get back on Buspar. That was the answer. I watched you be doped up all of my life, and I want no part of it! Why did everyone wait until I came here before telling me about my issues? I feel like no one has been honest with me. Is this how my life is going to be? Every time I screw up in life, is she just going to put me away? I don't understand why she couldn't have just left me alone like I told her.

I'm so sick of everyone saying, "Hang in there," "It'll be done before you know it," "I wish I could stay there for a week," and "You can do this." None of them have a freaking clue. None of them! Everybody can talk the talk, but who's walking the walk? Not any of them. I'm the one who's been ripped away from everything I have known. Am I feeling sorry for myself now? Probably.

I am so sick of people wanting to know me—to get inside my heart. There is nothing there for anyone to see. I don't need help. I just need people to leave me alone.

I can't stop thinking about Sandy. You remember him don't you? He's the tall, sandy-haired guy that led my Bible study group. I fell in love with his personality the first time I met him. There may not be a lot of safe men in my life, but Sandy is definitely one. He makes me want to be closer to Jesus. I can't watch him die. I can't watch this happening. Every time I look at him, I see you. The same doctor diagnosed you both with the same type of cancer, in the same week. He was supposed to be in recovery, and then we get a phone call that the cancer comes back. I don't get that. I can't stop thinking about you. If only you would have fought like Sandy. Is his fight over? I can't watch this. I don't want to be a part of any of it!

I keep reliving those three weeks of hell over and over again. Every day I said good-bye to you, wondering if that would be the day. I fed you through the feeding tube. I made sure your pain medications were pumped in at the same time every day. I sat by your side, just staring at you, desperately wanting to climb into the hospital bed and lay by your side. I wanted my daddy. Sometimes I think that was worse than your actual death. If I would have known that day I said good-bye to you at the hospital would have been the last day I saw you, there would have been so many things I would have said. I'm so mad at you for leaving the way you did. I guess, though, as Francis Chan says, "Frankly, it's not all about me." Thinking about that has me reliving those three weeks of hell with you over and over again.

December 17, 2009

I'm so tired of wrestling. When does it end? Psalm 13:2, "*How long must I wrestle with my thoughts and day after day have sorrow in my heart? How long will my enemy triumph over me.*"

Neil T. Anderson wrote in *Bondage Breaker* that it's important for us to know and believe who we are in Christ. Fran's told us that, too. Knowing and believing are two different things I suppose.

I know you didn't live long enough after coming to know Christ to believe who you were in Christ. I wonder how that would have changed your perspective. Why am I even asking that? I believe the easy ones:

- I am God's child
- I am united with the Lord and I am one spirit with Him
- I have been bought with a price: I belong to God (I struggle, however, to believe that)
- I am a saint
- I have been redeemed and forgiven of all my sins
- I am free forever from condemnation
- All things work together for good
- I can find grace and mercy to help in time of need
- I am a temple of God

Fran's crazy if she thinks I'm going to stand in front of the mirror and say that stuff out loud. I may not have been here long, but I've been here long enough to know I can just pretend I'm doing it and she'll back off. If I tell her I'm not doing it in front of the mirror, she'll make me do it.

I know I've got to start trusting God. I know that! I want to. I do, and then I don't. *Help me, God!*

I trust in you, Lord. I trust in you. I'm lonely and afflicted. Show me your ways, Lord. Teach me your paths. Forgive my iniquity, though it is great. Relieve the troubles of my heart and free me from my anguish. I know I need to get out of your way so you can teach me. I only want to be in your truth, and I know I'm not doing that. Forgive me for my thoughts. Thank you for the strength that I don't act on all the thoughts I have. I don't want all this pride. Humble me. Prune me even though it's going to hurt. Test me and know my anxious thoughts. See if there is any offensive way in me. Thank you for your love. Help me to believe you love me. Thank you that you're not a scorekeeper. Why do I feel lonely and afflicted? My heart is breaking. I know you are there. I know you are with me. Rid me of this anguish. Take it from the very depths of me. Help me to stop burying everything. Take these troubles from my heart. Rescue me, Lord, for I want no part of shame. My hope is in you. Protect me. Never let go. Redeem me from my troubles. Redeem me, Father.

January 1, 2010

Happy New Year! I must say that I am thrilled 2009 is over. This certainly has to be a better year. I would probably mark last year down as the most humbling year of my entire life.

You know what I have been learning about myself? I'm pretty dang prideful. Who knew, huh? Well, I guess I knew and was just in denial of that fact. Each day here seems to be more humbling. I spent Christmas with six women I had no idea would ever be in my business as much as they are. It was actually a great time, full of peace. But it was very humbling.

I have been humbled by the fact that everything I possess right now is in two boxes under my bed and one drawer in the bathroom. I'm learning to be okay with that.

The year 2009 was full of mistakes. I am learning that mistakes are okay, but it's when we refuse to admit those mistakes that we begin to get ourselves in trouble.

Admitting mistakes—that's something I'm going to try my hand at this year.

C.S. Lewis has been a great teacher to me regarding pride. He says in *Mere Christianity* that pride is the "great sin." I can't really disagree with that statement. "It was through pride that the devil became the devil. It is the complete anti-God state of mind." Wow! Nothing like being compared to the devil.

I don't want to be eaten up any longer by this spiritual cancer called pride. I do not want to go against the very thing that God hates. Yet I do; yet He forgives me. What a cool God! Lewis says, "If you think you are not conceited, it means you are very conceited indeed." There is a lot of truth in that statement. I can look at someone and absolutely detest their arrogance. But little do I realize, until God shows me in an embarrassing fashion, that I too am being arrogant. God detests haughty eyes. I want no part of that!

You don't realize how much you look down on others until you live with a person that is completely opposite of you twenty-four/seven. I didn't realize I did that so much until Fran was kind enough to point that out to me. (Insert sarcasm here). Really, though, it's true. Each one of us here has completely different personalities. I can't stand to watch one of the girls eat. I quickly find myself wrinkling my nose staring at her in disgust. There's another girl that takes forever to get the point across. I try to wait patiently, but I can only stand so many "ums" before wanting to slap her. I think to myself, *get to the point already!* That's not who I want to be. I don't want to destroy relationships because I'm being a judgmental, conceited brat.

Lewis says, "As long as you are proud you cannot know God. A proud man is always looking down on things and people: and, of course, as long as you are looking down, you cannot see something that is above you." It didn't hit me until I realized how bad my own insecurities were, that I've been looking down on others. Perhaps I was jealous of their security in themselves. I am learning to get myself out of God's way. He wants to use us all, but he can't when we are standing in his way. It is his personality I want.

I have had such an amazing reality check over the last month. It has been all about me, me, me. What about everyone else? What about their suffering? I have been convicted. I have spent much of the last month asking God's forgiveness for my selfishness. I want this year to be about others, not just myself. As Beth Moore says in the *Daniel Bible Study*, "The enemy is sly. He will try to take the very thing meant to instill humility and twist it into pride." I hate the pride I see in myself.

January 27, 2010

I am fighting the lies on believing that love is overrated. What does it really mean? I hear the word from so many people, but I don't believe it. How can people possibly love me? How do you know that someone really loves you?

Fran made me sit down and write a list of the people who love me. Really, I just wrote names down to appease her. My first mistake: I forgot to write her name down. Now she vows to tell me she loves me every day. We'll see. I had to go back and work on the list some more.

When I began to work on the list I thought to myself, *I can think of five or six people who really love me?* When my pen began to touch the paper the second time around, however, God kept showing me more. I didn't just see people in my memories saying those three words; I saw their actions showing true love.

I've carried this fear around for the last twenty-one years that no one could possibly love me. I have believed the lies that I didn't deserve to be loved; I wasn't worthy to be loved by anyone. Of course I went back to telling myself that if I could have been perfect you wouldn't have drank. If only I wouldn't have needed so much, Mom wouldn't have worked all the time. I have walked around in this life believing I was completely unlovable. After today, I have a strong, well-thought out, theological statement to describe those feelings. What a bunch of crap!

She had me write a list of people who don't love me also. I actually struggled. I thought for sure I wouldn't have any problems listing those names. I reached into the deepest parts of my heart, and a few names popped up. Two significant people came to mind, one being my third grade teacher. Then more names came to mind.

I wanted to make the list. I wanted to write down those who hurt me in my life. They didn't love me. My sexual abusers, they didn't love me. Then God tugged on my heart asking, "What if they don't know how to love?" I guess that's why he is God and I'm not. I couldn't write their names down. Maybe they really didn't know how to love.

So what do I do with that? I have already taken the first step—forgiveness. I guess now I get on my knees and pray for them. Yes, I may have bore the pain of their sufferings because of their lack of love, but instead of anger, I feel sorrow for their breaking hearts. If only they could see what Jesus could change in them. Maybe someday they will. I am reminded in Matthew 5:44 that I am to *"pray for those who persecute me."* If I love those who love me what reward do I get? I'm starting to get it.

I accept that you loved me. I know you did. I have to keep telling myself that. You always said the words. You never hesitated to tell me. I know that means something. I was just so hungry for your actions to show the same.

I used to sit and wonder if your actions would ever change. I would hear you say, "I love you" through the slurred words. Then you would hug me, and I could smell the Bourbon. After a while, I learned to let go of the expectations that you would ever show your love in another way.

Then some days you would surprise me. You would take the fish off my hook. You would cook me dinner. You would sit at the kitchen table with me and teach me how to play the spoons. You were the coolest person I ever knew when you played the spoons. When you baked bread, I could smell the scent of fresh oranges in the air. Those were the times it was just you. It was you and I. There was no whiskey, no drugs, and no sadness. Those days I felt your love. How I desperately want those days back. I can smell the orange bread right now.

I remember your action of love when I was in the hospital. You were there every day. You cooked for me.

You got me a warm washrag for my head. You held my hand. When I had to learn how to walk again, you were there. You kissed my head every day before you left. You pushed me around in a wheelchair with a proud smile on your face. I may have only been ten years old, but I saw it. You had a different glow on your face then.

Sometimes I find myself wishing that would have never ended. You were sober. I could count on you. You helped take care of me. For the first time in my life, I trusted that you were going to show up and be there for me. You did. I count two broken legs as a blessing. My daddy to be there, if only for a little while. You were there as you, not a broken person trying to hide his pain with alcohol.

The reality is setting in that for the first time in my life I am truly letting Jesus love me. I am allowing myself to enjoy the beauty he gave me; the way he made me. I feel his love like I have never felt it before.

I can't stop thinking about that day in the prayer room. I wish I could relive that moment every day. I was lying in the floor, with my hands stretched out, wondering once again, why I was here. I had fought so hard that day. I had fought against everything and everyone. Tears streamed down my eyes, and I was so desperate for answers, but I couldn't say anything. I didn't really have anything to say to God. I guess that's what he was waiting for, me to finally shut up long enough to hear him.

Then he spoke to me in the clearest, softest voice, "Sundi Jo, when are you going to let me love you?" I get chills writing about it. I have been so worried about others loving me that I haven't even let God love me. I have been tuning him out for so long. I guess when I think about it, it was a one-way relationship. I was afraid to let him love me. Anyone who had ever said they loved me hurt me. Why would I expect God to love me?

I feel blessed to sit here, knowing that he loves me enough to keep giving me second chances. Acceptance. It really is an amazing feeling. I accept love. I accept God's love.

I am learning something about God; He is always there. I don't have to wonder if He is going to show up. For the first time in my life I am truly letting Jesus love me. I know his love when he wakes me in the morning with a spectacular sunrise. I know his love when a stranger walks up to me and says, "You have the most beautiful eyes I have ever seen." I know his love when a friend tells me they can truly see me walking with Christ. I know his love when a sister comes up to me and says, "I want what you have. Will you pray with me?" God is loving me.

February 9, 2010

As more women come and go here, it seems there are several connections between us. Most of the women have been sexually abused. Most of them had horrible relationships with their fathers, and many of them have been involved in some type of homosexual relationship. Interesting. Perhaps now is the time to tell you that I struggled with it as well.

One of the definitions of *homosexuality*, according to Webster's Dictionary, is "a sexual attraction to persons of the same sex." What if it has absolutely nothing to do with being attracted to each other?

I'm sure you had to know or at least have your ideas. But I could never feel safe enough to tell you. I remember once when I was a little girl you told me that if I ever dated a black man or was gay, you would disown me. That always scared me, yet put rebellion in me at the same time. I dated a black man simply to spite you. But getting to know more of your heart before you died showed me that you previously said wasn't true. You would never have disowned me. Still it was better left a secret, in my opinion.

You should know that Jammie and I were together for five years. It was one of the hardest, craziest, safest parts of my life. It's definitely a story for a made-for-TV movie. Sometimes I look back and still can't believe that was part of my life.

Rewind to February 2002. I was an eighteen-year old, confused girl seeking answers. I partied every weekend with friends and family. I had just moved back from Nashville, and I was angry. Angry that I was back home. Angry that my aunt Terra was dying. Angry that Mom didn't understand me. Once again, you were out of my life. I was ready to be whatever anyone told me to be, just so I could fit somewhere.

Others would tell me, "You're gay, Sundi Jo. Just admit it." What if I was? What if I was just holding back out of fear? I hadn't had many relationships with men. They had all hurt me. Why would I want another one? What if men were all like you? I didn't want my heart broken time and time again. Perhaps I would be single for the rest of my life. Or I could pursue what others were telling me to do: homosexuality.

After a long night of partying with friends, I wound up at a bar a few towns away. There was a group of soldiers from Fort Campbell, Kentucky, playing pool. I had lots of liquid courage that evening and decided they needed to buy us all drinks. They did. By the end of the night, I had invited a few of them back to my apartment to continue the party.

I woke up the next morning with a horrible headache and a man whose last name I didn't even know. A rage filled me that I still can't explain. I quickly woke him up and forcefully told him to get out of my house. I'm sure he thought I was crazy. Maybe I was. All I knew was that I wanted him gone. I looked around the apartment at my friends passed out on various pieces of furniture. What had I done?

I took a shower to wash the shame away, but it was still there. There was no amount of soap to wash the disgust off. I locked myself in my bedroom, and the tears flowed. I hated myself. I hated the man I had slept with and would never see again. I hated every man that existed. I made a vow to myself that day. I would never again be with another man. The decision had been made, and I stuck with it.

The next weekend, in another drunken stupor, I kept my promise to myself. Jammie came for a visit, we partied all night, and the rest was history. Going through a bad breakup with her boyfriend of over five years, we both decided in a sort of silent agreement that we were done with men. Thus began a five-year relationship between two women who had been friends since high school.

I think we both knew from the beginning we were getting ourselves into a mess, but we had to go for it. Nothing else had worked. It would be the safest thing for both us. No more men could hurt us. We could count on each other and make it work. So we did. For a while.

Within a few months I moved to her hometown. We kept it from our families for about a year. I finally got tired of holding the secret, so I made the announcement. Most people accepted it, in front of me anyway. Mom struggled with it for a while. Why wouldn't she? Her only child has just dropped the bomb that she was gay. But I really didn't care how she felt about it. It was going to work for me.

In 2004 we moved to Branson, living life as normal. Normal to us anyway. We were happy. Life was great. We had a nice house. Great jobs. But unbeknownst to each other, we were both dying and miserable inside. We fought. We were completely different. We wanted different things in life. Jammie always wanted to be a mom. I wanted to be free to live life, though I didn't know what that looked like at the time.

Jammie was depressed all the time, and I was usually pissed off about something. We were miserable, but neither of us would admit it. Not only that, but staying faithful to each other didn't happen. Both of us despised men, but in our own ways we didn't completely allow ourselves to avoid them. We were both good secret-keepers. Life for us was a mess, but at the same time it was safe. Safe in an extremely, crazy way.

The longer we were together, the harder our hearts became. We barely communicated. We had become frustrated roommates, both afraid to speak up and tell each other how we were really feeling.

In 2005 things started to unravel, in a good way. We visited a church in December and fell in love with the atmosphere. Something about it felt different. A different kind of safe perhaps. We started serving in the church and vowed to keep our secret from others. In July 2006, after seven months of fighting God's call for me, I finally surrendered and gave my life to Christ. Jammie had done so not long before. Neither of us had any idea what that meant.

Something started happening to my heart, though. Something I had never experienced before. I was feeling guilty for my actions. I was feeling guilty for being unfaithful to a relationship that I didn't want to be in anyway. Truthfully, it was messed up. I wanted out. I wanted out desperately but didn't know how. Jammie wanted the same thing. It was as though we both knew what the other was thinking, but we couldn't bring ourselves to say it. Life had gotten too comfortable to be shaken up now.

The more we got involved in church, the worse it got. I would get around Ted B. and this thing called conviction would take over me. I was lying. I was living a life I didn't belong in. I was pretending everything was normal. I would go home on Sundays after church and cry. It was time to make a decision.

Instead of making the right decision, however, we decided to buy a house. I remember signing the papers with a heart full of regret. What was I doing? We were getting ourselves into a deeper mess, but neither of us had the courage to speak up.

Finally, in December things finally came to head. I woke up that morning and knew that something had to change that day. I watched Jammie pull out of the driveway to head to work that morning, and I could feel my heart breaking. I soon followed, driving away from the house we had only owned for two months. I prayed for God to show up. I begged him to show me what to do. Little did I know, He was planning to break me like never before.

I couldn't function at work that day. I couldn't think straight. I picked up the phone and told Jammie we needed to talk. She knew it was coming. I picked her up fifteen minutes later. We sat in my truck in the middle of the Target parking lot in silence. I wanted to speak, but I didn't know what to say. So did she. Our tears said everything, but we could say nothing.

"I can't live like this anymore," I finally told her. The conviction was killing me. I knew if I was going to do this Christianity thing that I had to make some changes. Ending this relationship was one of the first changes. Though I was scared to death, at the same time something felt so freeing to finally get it out. Almost five years of stuffing feelings had finally been released. We talked. We cried. We knew it was over. I drove her back to work.

When I got home that evening, I stepped into a house full of cold sadness. Neither of us could think of the right thing to say. Where did we go from there? For days we went back and forth from relying on our feelings to recognizing the truth, back to our feelings again. I knew for this to work I would have to stand firm in my decision. Not because Jammie didn't want to. She was just afraid. She had lived to please others all her life, and she didn't know what to do at this moment. She would have stayed miserable to stay safe, even if that meant being in a relationship she knew wasn't going to work if we were going to follow God's call. I was going to have to accept the position of bad guy.

A week later I lost my job. Then Christmas came. One of the loneliest days of my life was Christmas Eve of 2006. Jammie had gone to be with her family. I wasn't ready to be around mine. I sat in a new house filled with brand new furniture, unemployed, alone, and broken. For the first time in my life, I was on my knees in the middle of the floor crying out to God. I had finally made a much-needed decision, yet my world was crashing down on me. I didn't understand. Following God wasn't making sense to me.

I would love to say that things quickly got better. They just became worse. It came to the point of anger for both of us. Some truth began to surface, and we soon came to realize that it just might be impossible to maintain a friendship after this huge mess we had put ourselves through.

But I am a fighter. I was determined to keep fighting to save our friendship. We had never stopped being friends, and I wasn't about to just give up, regardless of what society was telling us. Besides, we were both stuck in this house together, trying to figure out how to pay for it since I no longer had a job.

We actually began to hate each other through the process of trying to mend our friendship. There was cussing, screaming , and a whole lot of crying. I made the decision to go to counseling. My control issues actually paid off. I was going to be in control of saving this friendship whether Jammie liked it or not. Most people go to counseling to save their marriage. We were going to figure out how we could end this messed up relationship and bring it back to the friendship that it had originally started out as.

We had breakthroughs. We had setbacks. We would take one step forward and three steps back. God definitely has a sense of humor, though. I ended up losing my truck, and we were forced to share a car. When you can't necessarily get away from each other, you can either make it worse or make it better. We tried both.

Finally we had the big breakthrough. We agreed we had a friendship that was worth saving, and though what we were going through may have looked crazy to the outside world, we knew God would restore it, if we would just let him. He restored it indeed. Today we have a stronger friendship than we ever had.

When you died, she never left my side. She sat with me at the funeral home, as I had to answer questions I didn't even know how to answer. She held my hand during your memorial service. I stood by her side as her maid of honor as she married her husband. She stayed by my side the day she broke the news to me that my grandpa died. Even though I had nothing to say, she was silent with me.

We've gone through things since I have been here at TRFC, but again, we worked through them because we know we have been to hell and back together, and we're not quitting anytime soon. I'm so grateful you got the chance to know her before you died. I am grateful to call her my best friend. I am grateful that I will be the world's greatest aunt to her children. I am thankful to Jesus for restoration, even when getting there is so painful.

I'm sorry I never told you about it, but I thought it was better you didn't know. I'm sure that was more my own fear and shame than anything to do with you. Something tells me you had an idea anyway. Thanks for loving me whether you knew or didn't. You never had as hard of a heart that you said you did. I get that from you.

February 15, 2010

Today you would have been forty-nine years old. It's hard to believe. I haven't been out of bed all day. I spent last night in the emergency room with a ruptured cyst. Valentine's Day turned into your birthday on a hospital bed. Way to celebrate, huh?

I remembered staring at the clock last night at midnight. Tears trickled down my cheek, and once again, Jammie was there to wipe them away. "Happy birthday to my daddy," I said.

I wonder how much safer I would have felt if you would have been there last night. Perhaps as safe as I felt when you were there through the car accident. I guess there really is nothing like having your daddy and his strength there for a little girl in some of her weakest moments. I miss you. I really do.

February 24, 2010

One year ago today you left. Some days it seems like yesterday. Some days it seems like years ago. Yesterday was one year since the last time I ever heard your voice. It was the last time I ever heard you say, "I love you." I wish I could hear you say it again and again. I relive the months leading up to your death a lot. I know someday I have to stop thinking about them, but it's hard.

I got a call the week before Christmas that you were dying. They said your lungs were full of fluid and Hospice was bringing you home to die. I was sitting in Jennifer's spare bedroom. They said you were refusing help and wanted to die. I was so mad at you. My fear of abandonment immediately kicked in, and I knew you were leaving me again, just like you always had.

I stayed in bed most of the day, only getting up when Jennifer told me I had to eat something. I couldn't really believe it was happening. I was making plans in my head to tell you good-bye and bury you. One minute I was so mad at you. The next, I was praying for God to save your soul. Later that night I realized it was up to me. I was going to have to bring you to Jesus before you died.

I drove to Belle the next day ready to say good-bye to you. When I walked in, you were lying in bed, and you looked so fragile. I just held your hand and said, "I'm here." You nodded your head and acknowledged I was there. I didn't know what to say. I didn't know what to do. This seemed like way too much vulnerability for you and I.

I told you about my week and all the things I was learning in my new Beth Moore *Breaking Free* Bible study. The next thing I knew I was on my knees beside your bed with my Bible in hand. I still don't remember how it got there. I remember asking you questions about Jesus, and for every question I asked, you would nod your head.

"Do you know that you can be forgiven for your sins?"

You nodded your head yes.

"Do you want to accept Jesus into your heart?"

You nodded your head yes.

"I'll say the prayer, then you say amen, okay?"

Again, you nodded your head yes.

"God, my dad knows that he has sinned, and that sin separates him from you. We both know and believe that Jesus Christ died for us. Dad wants to be forgiven for his sins. He wants you to come into his life. He wants you to be in charge of his life. Thank you for your forgiveness. Thank you that my dad knows you. In Jesus's name, Amen."

"Amen," you said. God gave you the strength to say that one word.

The hospital bed wouldn't be delivered until the next day. So, for the first time since I was a little girl, I would sleep with you. There I was, a twenty-five-year-old girl, curling up next to her forty-seven-year-old father. It was moments like these I longed for all of my life.

I couldn't sleep. I just kept staring at you, listening to you breathe. I put my hand on your chest as it went up and down with every breath. I think I memorized all the features of your face that night, knowing soon I wouldn't get to see them anymore. Then you put your arm around me. I don't know if you were even aware of it.

I felt so safe. I begged God to just keep it that way forever. I wanted to stay in that spot forever. I was a little girl again. It took me back to the one time I ever remember snuggling up with you. I was staying with you for the weekend. You were lying in bed watching a movie. I climbed up next to you and laid my head on your chest as you put your arm around me.

It was just us. The rest of the world didn't exist at that moment. It was a picture of heaven to me: a little girl wrapped up in the arms of her father. There wasn't the smell of whiskey or cigarettes. You smelled like what I always imagined a dad to smell like. I had never felt safer with you. You smiled at me and squeezed me tighter.

There I was again, twenty-five years old, picturing heaven with your arms around me. That must be how it's going to feel with God, huh? I will get to rest in his arms for eternity, feeling the safety I felt that day, forever. You, too. You get that, too. My little slice of heaven was interrupted the next morning by a knock on the door from the delivery of the hospital bed. The reality that you were dying was back.

The next three weeks were the longest weeks of my life. Every morning I told you I loved you and said good-bye. I rubbed your nasty man feet, brushed your hair, and even cleaned your fingernails. I slept in the chair next to you almost every night, listening for your breaths to change.

The days God gave you the strength to talk were the greatest days. You would smile and crack a joke. You would hold my hand and tell me you loved me. You were always reaching out for my hand. You needed me. I felt needed by you. There were days you still managed to be your cranky, old self, especially when it came time to decide whether it would be chocolate or strawberry Ensure in your feeding tube that day. I finally had to wait for you to fall back to sleep so you wouldn't fuss about it.

We planned your funeral together, and I finally let you convince me to cremate you. One of the greatest moments of those three weeks was being able to forgive you. I forgave you for not being there. I forgave you for hurting me. I forgave you for it all. You forgave me, too. You forgave me for pushing you away so much. You forgave me for refusing to be vulnerable with you. Thank you.

Every day the nurse would come in and say, "It could be any time." Doctor's orders were to give you pain medication around the clock. I did. As each day progressed, she would increase the amount of medication you got. Like clockwork, I inserted the meds into your tube. I just wanted to keep you comfortable. When you refused to eat, I stopped making you. There was no more Ensure. There was no more giving you tiny sips of root beer.

You got weaker and finally stopped talking. The days grew longer, as all you did was sleep. I would sit next to you and read the Bible. We managed to make it to 11:30 on New Year's Eve before I fell asleep holding your hand. We welcomed 2009 together. Then came the day.

The nurse came in to do her usual routine, just as I was doing mine. I made some oatmeal and sat down at the table with my banana. Then she said, "I don't think it will be long." My oatmeal didn't look so appealing anymore. She packed up her bags, gave me a sympathetic smile, and was out the door. I didn't leave your side. My arm was falling asleep, but I couldn't make myself let go of you.

As I was finally forcing myself to step away from you long enough that afternoon to eat something, another Hospice nurse showed up. That wasn't routine. After realizing she had made a mistake in the scheduling, she decided she would check you while she was there. As she put the stethoscope to your chest, she had an odd look on her face. I just knew she was going to tell me you were gone. She did the complete opposite.

"Your dad isn't dying," she said.

I took a double look. I had sat by you for three weeks and watched you get worse each day. There was no doubt you were dying.

"He's overmedicated. I think he is getting too much medication."

"He's getting the exact amount the doctor told me to give him," I said with a dazed look on my face.

She looked at the chart and gasped. "There is no reason he needs this much medicine. You are overmedicating him."

I burst into tears, trying to make sense of what she was telling me. I was killing you! I was doing everything I was told, and it was killing you. That was a divine appointment that day. I believe with all my heart that if that nurse hadn't showed up, that was the last day you would have been alive.

I immediately stopped your medicine, according to her advice. She was putting her job on the line by protesting the doctor's order, but I think your life was more important to her at that point.

Within two days you were coming to. You were opening your eyes. You were sitting up. I still can't wrap my mind around it really. You practically went from dead to alive within two days. You were talking to me. You were back.

I was celebrating on the outside but so confused on the inside. I finally lost it. I remember running out the door and getting in the car. I just needed to drive. I stopped at the park, slammed my hands against the steering wheel, and screamed at God, "What do you want from me?" I didn't know what else to say. I screamed as loud as I could. Then I went back home to you.

A couple days later I wrapped a jacket around you, grabbed your oxygen tank, and helped you get in the car. We rode gravel roads for a couple hours and talked. We talked about your salvation. I told you about things you had missed. I cried. You cried. I haven't been on a gravel road since.

The next day we packed you up and headed back to the hospital. You were alive. You were really alive! Your lungs were still full of fluid. You had pneumonia, and you were dehydrated. I sat with you for a bit and got you all settled in. I promised I would call every day and check on you. Before I left, I kissed your cheek. I kissed your forehead. I rubbed your hair. I hugged you. Then I left. It was the last time I ever saw you. Had I known, I would have crawled back into bed and never left my daddy's side.

On February 23 you called. We talked about fishing and riding some more gravel roads. I was coming to see you that week. You were out of the hospital. The pneumonia was better. We were going to have a great time. It was going to be the first time in our lives that things were really going to be different. Before we hung up you said, "I love you."

The next day you were dead. They said you died sitting up in the chair, just like you had fallen asleep. I just kept saying to Mom, "I don't understand! I don't understand!" I didn't. I had just talked to you. You were better. I was coming to see you in four days.

I never learned how you died. They didn't do an autopsy. They just assumed it was your cancer. I never got to see you again, as I respected your wishes of being cremated. The last memory I ever have of you alive is kissing your forehead in the hospital. I'd give anything to have it back.

Jammie drove me to the funeral home. She held my hand as I signed papers. Most of that day is a blur, but I remember she never left my side. Never. We had your memorial service a couple days later. I stood in the entryway to greet guests as they came in. Apparently that's what you're supposed to do. People hugged me. They gave me their condolences. I could smell whiskey on some of your old friends, mixed with the stench of cigarettes. They took their seats, and all I could do was stand there, trying to make sense of it all.

Ted B. was there, as promised, to direct the service. He told the story of your salvation. He talked to those in the crowd who were still living the life that you had been. He gave a message of hope, but he did it so directly. He didn't candy coat things. He let the lost know they were separated from God. At the end of the service he asked everyone to bow their heads. He then asked those who wanted to receive Christ to raise their hands, and he prayed the prayer of salvation.

Ted B. came up to me at the end of the service and said, "Sundi Jo, five people raised their hands." I smiled. I know Jesus was smiling. He said to me, "Your dad just did more in his death for others than he did in his life." That was true.

As I watched everyone file out to go on about their lives, I couldn't leave yet. The church was clear, and I shut the door. I sat in the front row with your ashes in my hands. I couldn't say anything. I could only sit.

It was then that I felt the tangible presence of God. I could feel his arms around me. The reality was that you were gone, but God wasn't. In a time of deep sadness, I felt an inexpressible joy, knowing that He was there.

Before leaving town to come back home to Branson I drove by my grandpa's house. I wanted to go in and hug him, but I wouldn't allow myself to. You looked just like him. You shook your leg like him. You drank your coffee like him. You cussed like him. He was your twin, just with whiter hair. I knew without a doubt that at your memorial service that day, that would be the last time I ever talked to my grandpa again. I was right. I never called him. I never wrote.

Six months later I got the phone call that he had died. Jammie came to bring me the news, and I had no response. I stared at the ceiling. I let a teardrop fall, and then I dried my eyes. I rolled over in my bed and went to sleep. I had already been pretending that your death didn't really happen. I wasn't about to allow myself to face the reality that he had just died as well.

At his funeral I didn't speak much. I caught myself crying, refusing to allow others to see it, and once again, dried up the tears. I left the funeral home that day, got in the car, and headed home. Ten days later I was living here. Crazy how things work, huh?

Some days I still get mad at you for leaving. But today I'm not. Today I am just rejoicing that I get to see you again. I am thanking God that He gave me the strength to face my fear and talk to you about Jesus. Because of that bold step, I will see you again in eternity.

Until then, I love you.

March 3, 2010

I officially finished my list of fears today. Who knew it would take four months to work through a list of things I was scared of? You can put me down in the history books of one of the biggest scaredy-cats in human history.

- Fear of never being loved
- Fear of failure
- Fear of rejection by other people
- Fear of marriage
- Fear of being victimized
- Fear of disapproval
- Fear of going crazy
- Fear of the future
- Fear of the death of a loved one
- Fear of becoming/being homosexual
- Fear of being raped
- Fear of Mom
- Fear of my grandmother
- Fear of Jennifer
- Fear of Jammie
- Fear of never getting married
- Fear of success
- Fear of being skinny
- Fear of men
- Fear of humiliation

I constantly find myself in the midst of my fear of humiliation, especially when I try and step out of my comfort zone. I went on a visiting pass for the weekend and agreed to wear a pair of large, hoop earrings. The moment a friend noticed them I tensed up and could feel the fear welling up inside of me. I waited for the jokes to come. They never did.

Allowing myself to feel humiliated has been a normal thing in my life. I was humiliated in the third grade when my teacher, Mrs. Baker, sat me in the middle of the class while the other students made snorting sounds like pigs at me. I had to grow up with all of those kids. Still to this day when I hang around them, I find myself waiting to be made fun of again. I wonder how many of them really remember it. I usually do something funny to make them laugh and try everything possible to avoid serious conversation with them, or allow myself to be vulnerable.

It wasn't just once my teacher humiliated me. Maybe once wouldn't have been so bad. Some days she refused to let me eat lunch. Other days she made me sit in the principal's office and eat because she said I was too fat to sit with my classmates. I feel humiliated just writing about it. I just want to ask her what she was thinking when she did those things. Where was her heart?

I can see where my fear of humiliation has caused me to want to be in control. If I'm in control, I can't be hurt. I look back in astonishment as I realize how much of my life has revolved around being in control. I decided at a very young age I had to be in control. It was the only way I would be safe.

I've never told you these stories. I've barely told anyone. In high school I had a blind date. I didn't really want to go, but a friend talked me into it. We decided we would both drive because he lived farther away, and it would work out better. Halfway there he pulled over. He told me he changed his mind, and it was all a joke. He told me I was too fat. I drove home humiliated and sobbing. I built another wall around my heart that day.

Isn't it amazing how your fears can go back to your childhood? The course of my life was paved because of the things that happened to me as a little girl. I often wonder how different things would be if I had talked about it then. Oh well. No need to live in the past anymore right?

I often felt your love for alcohol kept you from loving me. That is where the fear of never being loved came from. My fear of failure has told me for years that I would never be successful because I didn't deserve anything good. My fear of success told me I shouldn't try to accomplish things, because I would just mess them up anyway. Fran tells me that when I complete this program, my fear of success will no longer exist. It makes sense.

Need I explain my fear of marriage? I've never seen what a real marriage is supposed to look like. My grandparents' is a mess. My parents' marriage certainly can't be normal. We know how it turned out with you and Mom. Are my friends doing it right? I don't know what it's supposed to look like. I think it will be a fear I battle until the day I actually step up to the altar. I go back and forth between the fear of marriage and the fear of never getting married. But God's Word comforts me. *"For I know the plans I have for you," declares the LORD, "plans to prosper you and not to harm you, plans to give you hope and a future"* Jeremiah 29:11.

My fear of going crazy doesn't need much explaining. I already went there and now I know what steps to take to make sure I don't go back there. It certainly was not my favorite place to be.

Fran says my fear of men is something I won't be able to conquer until after I complete the program since there's not really a man around the house. But I have to believe it starts with you again. I was always afraid of you. I was afraid of your reaction when you drank. I was afraid to make you mad. I was afraid to trust you.

After being abused by men and struggling with my distant relationship with you at the same time, I came to believe the lie that all men were out to get me. Of course, having it engrained in my mind from Mom didn't help either. That has been a thought pattern that's seriously glued onto my heart.

I would assume my fear of rape was due to the constant nightmares I had. After having a dream, I would spend the next few days looking over my shoulder at every turn. I was constantly jumpy. I didn't want to be hugged. I didn't want to be touched. By the time I would recover from that dream, another would come.

However, the fear has gotten better since Fran has taught me to normalize my dreams. It's the coolest thing! When I wake up each morning, and if I've had the dreams, I have to tell myself that they do not define who I am. I then "normalize" it, as if it's just like going to the circus. Within five minutes of waking up,

I've completely forgotten about it and can go on with my day.

I have learned that fear is a lack of trust. Actually, when you think about it, it's a big slap in the face to God. I've learned that if I focus on God, I relieve the fear.

I remember you telling me a story once about being a little boy. You were in the bathtub when your mom came in screaming at you. She had a large mirror in her hand, and she broke it over your head. I think about that often. You were in such a vulnerable state and you got hurt, not only physically, but your heart as well. Yet when I would watch you two interact, you never disrespected her. Even after what she did to you, you still respected her. Was that out of fear? Were you still that little boy, afraid that she was going to hurt you again? Did you want to please her because of the fear she wouldn't love you?

Fear is a horrible disease I think. It keeps you from having deep relationships. It's a prison you keep yourself in. It's a trap full of lies that you convince yourself you can't escape. I hate it!

I remember Lauren telling Katie a story once. She was describing a puppy in a cage. It's frightened and doesn't know whether or not it should come out into the world. Its owner must gently instruct the dog that it's okay to come out of the cage. The door is open and the owner just waits. Tori chimed in and said, "Katie, how long will you sit in the cage with the door wide open?"

I don't know how that impacted Katie, but it changed my life. For years I had been sitting in a cage that I created, with the door wide open. I could walk out at any time, yet my fear kept me from doing so. Not anymore.

I don't have a spirit of fear. I have power and love and a sound mind.

March 7, 2010

I don't have words today. I have thoughts. I have images that keep turning in my head, but the words won't seem to come. Just when I thought I was digging into the details here and working through everything, God slapped me upside the head with something new. I desperately want to run. I want to hide. I want to believe the thoughts that this isn't real, but I know it is. I know it's far too real.

I started to process with the girls today, but I still couldn't get the truth to completely come out. It's all too much! Jennifer visited today, and, of course, she wanted to talk about it. What was I supposed to say?

Last weekend during one of my weekend passes I sat on her couch and told secrets I didn't even know were inside me. How does that happen? How could I possibly bury something so deep that one day it just pops back into my mind? I know it's all God's timing. I know he prepared me for the moment, but right now that's not making it easier.

She was trying to get me to say the word out loud during her visit today, and I couldn't bring myself to do it. I couldn't even bring myself to look her in the eyes. "What does all this mean?" I asked her.

"It means you were raped."

I can't stand the word. If I say it, things will be far too real. I'm not ready for that.

I am still thinking of the relief that came last Saturday from telling her. But I didn't even know I was telling her. It was like the words rolled off my lips without my knowledge, without me giving them permission. I collapsed in her lap and went to sleep, having no idea I would be here today scared to death and confused, wishing it was a dream.

I sat at TCBY with Jammie and shared the news. It was just in random conversation like a robot talking. Again, it just rolled off my lips, but the reality wasn't there. At that moment, it was just words. I could see the want to in her eyes to say something to me, but I think she was just as speechless as me.

I'm exhausted trying to grieve over this situation. I want to grieve it and get it over with. My mind is playing tricks on me and holding me back. Was my denial really that thick? I can't stop second-guessing myself. I have to start talking about it, I know.

I had just turned thirteen, I think. James and his brother came over to visit that night. My parents were out of town. It wasn't unusual for them to come over. They did all the time. We were smoking and drinking. I don't remember how much we had to drink, but I'm assuming it was quite a bit since I don't remember that well.

I remember saying good-bye and thinking they had left. I went to my room to go to sleep, or pass out I guess you could say. My head felt so heavy. I was getting moved around, but I couldn't wake up. I knew someone was on top of me. Slowly I was waking up, but I had no strength. Through the muffled sounds I recognized James's voice. He was starting to have sex with me, but I couldn't fight him. I could barely wake up or move.

I heard another voice yelling. It was his brother. The yelling got louder, and then he wasn't on top of me anymore. I could hear things being ruffled around, then the voices were gone. I don't remember anything else. I don't remember getting dressed or even waking up the next day. I don't remember anything, and I hate it!

What am I supposed to feel? I feel ashamed. So ashamed of myself. How could I let that happen? I want to ask so many "what ifs?." I feel dirty. I feel violated. This couldn't have really happened to me.

How could I have buried it for so long? I convinced myself it didn't happen, that's how. Does this explain the fear of rape I've had all my life? I guess that would make sense. It's been a legitimate fear because it happened, and I didn't even recognize it. For years I've dreamed about that fear. I've been raped in my dreams so many times. They've played in my mind for so long it's like I've just expected the dreams to come true. Little did I know, it really did happen.

I saw him three years ago. I talked to him, and it never came to my mind. Was I just in survival mode? What do I do with that? I don't want this to be real!

Please take it back, God! Please make it never have happened. Please take it away!

Why did it have to come back up? Why couldn't I just keep it buried? Keeping it buried wasn't hurting me. Remembering it now is what's hurting. I know I have to go through this pain, but it hurts so badly!

I'm choosing to forgive him. I have to make that choice right now, regardless of my feelings. It's not for him; it's for me. I pray for his soul. I can pray for him. I can forgive him. But how do I heal? I want to be healed. I want the shame to be gone.

March 8, 2010

I spent the morning in Fran's office. God has a funny way with his timing. I walked in to ask a question and just broke. She saw pain written all over my face, asked me how I was doing, and I lost it. I asked God for help yesterday and he showed up pretty quickly.

Though I'm still feeling a little awkward about this morning, I'm feeling so relieved as well. Fran and I did inner child work. Writing it out sounds weird I know, but it was very powerful.

She asked me if I was feeling angry with myself. Of course I was. How could I have let that happen? It was my fault. I deserved it. She said I had to forgive myself. She said I needed to tell the thirteen-year-old inside of me that it was okay. So I did, hesitantly.

I went back there. Back to what I could remember. I allowed myself to see me as the teenager that was scared to death. The girl that felt unsafe. I saw her in the bedroom crying. I saw her tears, and my heart broke. I wanted to take her hand, but I couldn't. I felt too much shame. Too much guilt. I let that happen to her. How could I comfort her?

Before I could protect the girl, I had to forgive myself as the adult. It wasn't my fault I couldn't protect her. I'm okay now. I'm okay today. He can't hurt me today. He can't hurt me anymore. He won't hurt me anymore.

Fran held my hand and said, "You can do this, Sundi Jo. You are okay, and you have to believe it." So I told myself out loud, "I am okay. Shame does not belong to me. I am forgiven. I choose to forgive myself. I am safe now."

I saw myself as a child again, still scared and waiting. This time I was able to reach out to her. I apologized for not protecting her but promised that I would now. I promised she was going to be okay. I could see myself grabbing her hand, and it was like a piece of the puzzle was connected.

I opened my eyes and looked at Fran. I really was okay. I felt relief. I was done avoiding. I *am* done avoiding. I'm ready to make it through this grieving process. I'm ready. I look like Rocky Balboa after losing a boxing match today from the swollen eyes, but I'm ready. I am safe tonight, and tomorrow is a new day.

I always assumed that rape was associated with some violent crime—that in order to claim it as that, some random stranger is supposed to break into your house, beat you up, and then force himself upon you. That's the way it's played out in the movies anyway. How could I possibly associate it with a "friend" of mine taking advantage of a young teenager who had too much to drink?

March 13, 2010

Mom came today for a mother-daughter workshop. I took her into the prayer room tonight and told her about the rape. I felt completely stupid the whole time I was telling her about it. Satan's lies keep telling me it's not real. She cried a little and then dried her tears. She had to be strong I guess, like she always does, but I know she's really not that strong. I pray she is able to grieve it and not have guilt.

I get that urge to be strong and not look fragile to others from her I would assume. I never really got to see that side of you. She wants to be tough on the outside. We both do, but inside we're soft and melting. We both want to be in control of our emotions and don't like it when we're not. God is making a breakthrough, though.

I know God is going to use what happened to me for his glory. His Word says so. I want to be at that point of complete obedience to do what he wants with it. I want to be able to share with other victims how I overcame that part of my past and am living in victory to tell about it.

I want to be obedient to you, Father. Teach me how.

April 6, 2010

I am exhausted, both emotionally and physically. I have nothing left in me. I spent two hours of my day in a stare-down with Fran. Well, I can't say it was two complete hours of silence. I should add the part of standing at a close enough distance for our noses to touch, while we screamed at each other. Is it crazy that

I'm not really sure what it was all about? One minute I was fine. The next, I was screaming.

I guess the last laugh is on me. I spent the rest of the day on a silence fast. I have to give kudos to God on that one. Way to keep my mouth shut!

I lost my team leader privileges today. What does that mean? I won't be driving the girls around anymore. I won't be making a grocery list. I won't be responsible for calling everyone out every five minutes. I won't be responsible for checking chores. I think I am okay with that—most of it anyway. Today has been an extremely humbling day.

Lord, I need your help. I don't know how everything got this way. How can I be okay one minute and completely going off the handle the next? I have made myself look like a complete fool in front of those that looked up to me. I need your strength, because I can't do it on my own. Help me. Please help me.

April 07, 2010

I have spent more hours in the prayer room this week alone than I have since coming here in August, and it's only Wednesday. I have barely spoken a word to others in the house. I locked myself in the prayer room for hours asking God to change my heart. I refused to come out until he did. I wasn't leaving that room until I had a clear understanding of love and why it's so important.

The *Student Bible Dictionary* defines *love* as "a deep, enduring concern for others' welfare; affection; friendship." It is also defined as an essential characteristic of God that comes only as a gift. So love is an essential characteristic of God.

If love is essential to God, then it must be to us as well right? We are required to love; it's not an option. Must we love everyone, or just those we choose to love? In Matthew 5:43-36 Jesus said, *"You have heard that it was said, love your neighbor and hate your enemy. But I tell you: Love your enemies and pray for those who persecute you, that you may be sons of your father in heaven…if you love those who love you, what reward will you get?"* Oh, if only it were that easy to do. Fran says following Christ is not easy. She's got that one right.

How can you love those who you feel are against you? How do you love your enemies? How do you turn the other cheek after being struck once? The Pharisee's taught in Leviticus 19:18 that you should love only those who love in return. They implied elsewhere that you should hate your enemies. But Jesus says differently.

Not only does Jesus command us to love our enemies, we must bless them as well. We must *"pray for those who mistreat us"* (Luke 6:28). He goes onto say that *"even sinners can love those who love them* (Luke 6:32). If you love your enemies then you are truly doing Christ's work.

This is not easy, nor is it something all are willing to do. It is possible for only those whose lives are fully surrendered to God. We can only show love to those we may not necessarily feel love for through the power of the Holy Spirit. Without our Father's guidance we are simply selfish, sinful creatures roaming this Earth. We cannot do it by our own power.

What I find amazing is that God still loves those who hate him. He loves those who spit in his face. He loves those who curse his name. He loves those who turn their backs on him. Not only does he love; He patiently waits for their return.

"For God so loved the world that he gave his one and only Son, that whoever believes in him shall not perish but have eternal life" (John 3:16). I love how *The Message* puts it: *"This is how much God loved the world: He gave his Son, his one and only Son. And this is why: so that no one need be destroyed; by believing in him anyone can have a whole and lasting life."*

I had to consider putting myself in this position for a moment. I am picked out of a crowd to be a follower. Out of an entire population I am picked as one of the twelve people to sit next to Jesus and know him on a deeper level than most. I am trusted enough to be put in charge of all the disciples' funds. I witness miracles every day and sit by the fire each night, listening to Jesus speak wisdom, truth, and love. How could I be so lucky?

Then greed takes over my heart. The Pharisees wave a few bucks in my face for the trade of turning Jesus in. I begin to imagine what I am going to spend the money on. My thoughts are quickly interrupted as I realize it's time for dinner with Jesus and the other disciples.

My stomach is full, and I can't help but smile, as I know my pockets will be full soon as well. The man I am about to betray walks over to me and gently washes my feet. Think about that for a second. He is my teacher. My leader. My Savior. He gets on his knees and washes my dirty feet. Do I feel the slightest bit guilty? "What you are about to do, do quickly," Jesus says. God loves us despite what he knows about us or what we're about to do.

I head out the door prepared to betray him. I've got the money in my pocket, and Jesus has a crown of thorns around his head, after expressing his love for me and washing my feet. He is beaten beyond recognition. Every drop of blood he sheds is because of his love for me. Each time the nail is hammered into his hands, he loves me more. And as he hangs on the cross and draws his last breath, he still loves me, even though I turned the other cheek. That's love.

I am learning that when you truly love someone, you must be willing to give beyond what you know, including self-sacrifice. Our love must be like Jesus's. Am I a true disciple and follower or an uncommitted pretender? If I do not love everyone—not just the ones who are easy to love—then I am just pretending. I don't want to be fake. I can only be a true disciple if I really show the love God shows me. Why does it have to be so hard?

"If you hold to my teaching, you are really my disciples" (John 8:31). What did Jesus teach? *"Love the Lord your God with all your heart and with all your soul and with all your mind. This is the first and greatest commandment. And the second is like it: 'Love your neighbor as yourself'"* (Matthew 22:37-39).

This doesn't just mean our friendly, smiling neighbors. It means giving deep love to those who test our patience every moment we are around them; those who get under our skin like an annoying splinter. *"By this all men will know that you are my disciples, if you love one another"* (John 13:34). My interpretation: "All people will know you follow me and love me by the way you love the splinters under your skin."

We are to love others based on Jesus's sacrificial love for us. What happens if we love like Jesus? Will it bring unbelievers to Christ? It is starting to sound worth it. We are called to be living examples of Jesus's love.

Love isn't just a word. It is an action. 1 Corinthians 13:4-7 says, *"Love is patient, love is kind. It does not envy, it does not boast, it is not proud. It is not rude, it is not self-seeking, it is not easily angered, it keeps no record of wrongs. Love does not delight in evil but rejoices with the truth. It always protects, always trusts, always hopes, always perseveres."*

I am realizing that those aren't merely words to me anymore. It requires action. It is only possible to practice this love with God's help. When I put myself aside and let him do the work, the more I become like Christ. That is the ultimate goal and purpose of my mere existence.

"Love must be sincere...be devoted to one another in brotherly love. Honor one another above yourself...be joyful in hope, patient in affliction, faithful in prayer. Share with God's people who are in need. Practice hospitality. Bless those who persecute you...live in harmony with one another. Do not be proud, but be willing to associate with people of low position. Do not be conceited" (Romans 12:9-16).

God is calling me to be real, to have sincere love. What does real look like? It is speaking truth with grace. It's not holding back for fear of hurting others' feelings. It's having true compassion. I have to stop pretending I care and *really* care. True love is what I want so badly.

My love seems to be like a toggle switch. I can turn it on when I am in the right mood but often flip it off if it's not suiting to me. This is where I have to shift from being a people-pleaser to a God-pleaser. This is a hard road to walk.

I can't truly love if I am still holding grudges. God warns, *"Bear with each other and forgive"* (Colossians 3:13). He continues, *"and over all these virtues put on love, which binds them all together in perfect unity. And regardless of what else you put on, wear love. It's your basic, all-purpose garment. Never be without it"* (MSG). My garment needs a lot of work.

Loving is the most difficult thing to do, in my opinion. Maybe that's why it is the greatest commandment. Love looks like humility. When pride exists you have put loving others on the back burner. God says it cannot work that way. We must *"clothe ourselves with humility toward one another"* (1 Peter 5:5). Jesus himself was *"gentle and humble in heart"* (Matthew 11:29).

Love is grace. Rick Warren calls it courtesy. We are to *"be big hearted and courteous"* (Titus 3:2 MSG). We are to be courteous to those "different" people. Warren calls them EGR people—"Extra Grace Required." Why does this have to be so difficult for me? Katie is an EGR. She's been a thorn in my side since the moment I got here. Every roommate here drives you nuts in one way or another, but Katie has provided more opportunities for me to show patience than I can count. Let's just say I've failed miserably many times.

Father, help me see Katie as you see her. I want to see her through your eyes. I know that is the only way I can love her the way I am supposed to. Help me to pray for her. Show me how to love her. Love her through me. Take away my judgment. I don't want it. I want to love her. I want to give her grace. Help me to stop trying to love her on my own. It's wearing me out. It is making me someone I know I am not. Help me!

Love is loyalty. Love is complicated and requires patience. I am well aware God has put Katie in my life as a sharpening tool. She helps me to grow. She should feel lucky that I have been in the prayer room for the past seven hours. I want to love her. I want to.

April 20, 2010

God smacked me with truth today. I was sitting on the couch reading the Bible and opened it to this verse: 1 Thessalonians 5:14, *"Encourage the timid, help the weak, be patient with everyone."* My footnotes say, "Don't yell at the timid and weak; encourage and help them." At times it can be difficult to distinguish between idleness and timidity. Two people may be doing nothing—one out of laziness and the other out of shyness or fear of doing something wrong. The key to ministry is sensitivity: sensing the condition of each person and offering the appropriate remedy for each situation. You can't effectively help until you know the problem. You can't apply the medicine until you know where the wound is.

Sensitivity. I'm lacking it. I cannot do God's work if my heart isn't tuned into other people. I can't just pretend. It wears me out, and I become judgmental, prideful, arrogant, and bitter. Sensitivity is the key to ministry.

"A new command I give you: Love one another. As I have loved you, so you must love one another. By this all men will know that you are my disciples, if you love one another" (John 13:34-35).

April 29, 2010

Gary Smalley came to chapel tonight. I seriously love that man and have to wonder why of all the things he could be doing with his time, he chooses to invest time into us girls. People from all over the world seek him out for advice, and there he sat this evening, surrounded by all of us, who could give nothing back to him. We could only take.

He told me tonight that I was going to write a book. He said when I graduate from here, he's going to help me get started. If I wasn't in such a bad mood I might just believe him.

He introduced these thoughts to us tonight. I think he just might be onto something. He called them the purple beliefs versus the red beliefs. The purple beliefs are negative, and the red are positive. Each belief has at least one scripture to back it up.

The first belief (negative thought) is pride. Proverbs 11:2 says, *"When pride comes, then comes disgrace, but with humility comes wisdom."* The opposite of pride is humility. James 4:6 says, *"God opposes the proud but gives grace to the humble."*

The second negative thought is to love the world. 1 John 2:15-17 says, *"Do not love the world or anything in the world. If anyone loves the world, the love of the Father is not in him. For everything in the world—the cravings of sinful man, the lust of his eyes and the boasting of what he has and does—comes not from the Father but from the world. The world and its desires pass away, but the man who does the will of God lives forever."*

The opposite of loving the world is to love God. *"Love the Lord your God with all your heart and with all your soul and with all your mind and with all your strength"* (Mark 12:30).

The third negative belief is that you are to serve yourself. Philippians 2:3 says, *"Do nothing out of selfish ambition or vain conceit, but in humility consider others better than yourselves."* The opposite of serving yourself is serving others, just as Galatians 5:13-14 says to do. *"You, my brothers, were called to be free. But do not use your freedom to indulge the sinful nature; rather, serve one another in love. The entire law is summed up in a single command: 'Love your neighbor as yourself.'"*

The last negative thought is that all trials are bad. Proverbs 1:7 says, *"The fear of the Lord is the beginning of knowledge, but fools despise wisdom and discipline."* The opposite thought, of course, is that all trials are good. According to Romans 5:3-5, *"We also rejoice in our sufferings, because we know that suffering produces perseverance; perseverance, character; and character, hope. And hope does not disappoint us, because God has poured out his love into our hearts by the Holy Spirit, whom he has given us."*

Gary challenged us to say these verses out loud at least seven times per day. If we do, he said they would stay on our heart and start to change our lives. Why not give it a try? Honestly, I have nothing to lose by memorizing some scripture. I don't know about this whole seven times a day thing, but I think I'll give it a shot.

Give me the strength, Father. If this will change my life I want to do it. In Jesus' name, amen.

April 30, 2010

This has been one of the most challenging, life-changing months of my life. To say that I learned more about humility would be an understatement. This has probably been one of the quietest months of my time here. I have not been the biggest fan of words lately. God has been working on me with stillness. Part of that stillness for me has been to keep my big mouth shut and listen. I would say it's paying off.

My prayers lately have been prayers of desperation. I've been asking God to help me to continue to walk in humility. I want to walk in his ways. I want to be known as his disciple. I want to take my eyes off myself and put them on God. I want to walk in his footsteps. I want to be grateful for all that I have. Oh, how I haven't done that.

There were days all I could do was simply put one foot in front of the other. I was too tired to fight with my pride. I was too tired to keep going that way.

Fran and I are settled. I'd be lying if I said it didn't take a while on both of our parts. We finally apologized to each other. We hugged. We even said, "I love you." For the first time in a while, I walked out of her office with a sense of peace, despite the eleven demerits I got for my stinking pride. I picked up rocks, picked up sticks, wrote four papers, did two more silence fasts, cleaned the utility room, cleaned up dishes, and I don't remember what else. But you know what showed me I did it in humility? I kept a smile, knowing it could have been worse.

Beth Moore also told a story in the *Daniel* study that explains so much about my time here at TRFC. It is a story I hope to keep with me forever. King Nebuchadnezzar was a king in love with himself. Every great thing that happened in his kingdom he took credit for. He had a dream. He saw a huge tree in the middle of his land. It kept growing and touched the sky. It had beautiful leaves, abundant fruit, and was covered with food for every living thing. Animals found shelter, and the birds lived in the branches. According to Daniel 4:12, *"from it every creature was fed."*

"There before me was a messenger, a holy one, coming down from heaven. He called in a loud voice: Cut down the tree and trim off its branches; strip off its leaves and scatter its fruit. Let the animals flee from under it and the birds from its branches. But let the stump and its roots, bound with iron and bronze, remain in the ground, in the grass of the field" (Daniel 4:13-15).

Just as Daniel interpreted the dream, it was so. King Nebuchadnezzar was driven away from the people and sent to live with the wild animals. For seven years he grazed in a field like an animal until he renounced his sins. But, in the end, Nebuchadnezzar *"raised his hands toward heaven, and his sanity was restored. Then he praised the Most High; I honored and glorified him who lives forever"* (Daniel 4:34). He was restored.

I may not be grazing in a field, eating grass, with fingernails as long as a Ram's horn, but my tree was trimmed down to a stump. My pride was part of the cause. God cut Nebuchadnezzar's tree down, but he left the stump and roots. Not only that, but he covered them in bronze and iron. He protected the stump because he knew eventually, I think, that the king would be humbled again and come back to him.

I had to become a stump again. I am still a growing tree, covered in God's protection while He flourishes me. Someday soon I will be a strong, tall tree that bears beautiful fruit and feeds others with the gifts God has given me. Someday I will say, "I was once but a stump, but now I am a fruitful, beautiful tree."

May 8, 2010

I think today has been one of the most memorable days of my time here. It's hard to explain. Tonight I felt more real and free than I ever have. Jennifer came by for a surprise visit. It wasn't about trying to please her; it was about just simply being there. It's really hard to put words to.

When I was around you I could never be myself. I thought I couldn't anyway. I wanted to be whoever I could be for you to love me. That's how I have lived my life for so long. With you. With almost everyone. Today brought freedom.

For the first time in our friendship, I made eye contact long enough to realize she had green eyes. That may sound like a small step for some, but for me that was huge! My insecurities were wiped away. The focus wasn't on me and what I needed to change. It was on God and how we could glorify him in our conversations.

I've been doing the Gary Smalley thoughts. He was right. If I stick with memorizing and repeating those scriptures, my life will change. It already has. In a matter of nine days, I feel this peace like I've never felt before. My pride isn't puffed up. My confidence is in a place I didn't know it could be.

I told Jennifer about them tonight and just what they're doing for me. I told her the story of holding my tongue in our group session the other day when another person was trying to falsely accuse me of some things. While she was talking, I simply repeated out loud to myself, "With pride comes disgrace, but with humility comes wisdom." It was amazing! I didn't interrupt. I let her speak. I kept my pride back, and then I gently answered. I want to call Gary and tell him what happened.

Tonight we sat and talked about God, all the ways he is working, and how much he loves me. It's not just words coming from my mouth. It's truth coming from my heart. I am loved by a God who desires a relationship with me, a God who created me to do great works for him. I feel like I'm finally on that path.

Jennifer used a great word to sum up what I'm feeling. She said it was *peace*. Yeah, that's it. It's peace. It's that peace that passes all understanding. I finally have it. Finally.

Tomorrow I will wake up with the same desire I had today. The desire to be real. To be at peace. To serve the God who loves me.

Thank you, Father, for your strength. Thank you for the strength to run on the treadmill. I feel closer to you when I'm running, because I know I have to depend on you. I never want to be in a place where I don't depend on you. I'm sorry for my times of ungratefulness. You are my comfort, my strength, and my peace.

May 19, 2010

It seems my need to be in control is coming to an end. My name is Sundi Jo, and I am a recovering control freak. This week I have been working on my issues with authority. Come to find out, it's not normal to cuss out your teachers, high school principal, bosses, or any other authority for that matter.

Fran has had me working on digging into the past and figuring out where my issues with authority started. I wasn't sure I was ready for it, but apparently God thought I was. I would never have thought I could trace the exact day in the history of my life where this problem started. I never told you, but I guess there is no time like the present.

When I was being sexually abused, obviously, I had no control over that. The abuse stopped finally when I was eight years old. The damage had already been done, though. My authority had hurt me and lied to me in more ways than one. You, as my authority, were never around. When you were I didn't know what respecting you looked like, especially as I got older. When I became a teenager, I had no respect for you as my dad or my authority. To be honest, why would I? You never set an example for me. But I am learning that I was wrong. I still needed to honor you, even when you weren't necessarily honoring me. I'm sorry.

I was eight years old the day my view of authority completely shifted. I was in the third grade, and Mrs. Baker was my teacher. From the outside, she looked like your average teacher. She looked like a teacher was supposed to look. She was beautiful and wore these long, denim dresses and always had lipstick on. From the moment Mrs. Baker laid eyes on me, it seemed like my life was a living hell.

I was the fat kid in the class, and she made that apparent to all the other students around me. She never hid her disgust with me. I felt fear well up inside of me every time her eyes met mine. It wasn't like the fear I had with my first grade teacher, who tied me and another classmate up with a jump rope. Mrs. Baker's verbal abuse seemed to be worse than a jump rope. Being tied up only hurt me physically. The words of Mrs. Baker made me feel pain in my heart.

I remember the day the humiliation officially started. Mrs. Baker wanted to play a game. She called it "Pig in the Pot." All the students sat in a circle around the floor. Not me. Guess who got to be the pig? I had to stand in the circle while all the kids oinked at me.

These were kids I was growing up with. Kids I played foursquare on the playground with. They were simply respecting their authority and doing what they were told, oinking at the fat kid in the middle.

I ran home that day humiliated. I tried to think of ways I could avoid ever going back to school. I wanted to move. I convinced myself I couldn't tell anyone. No one would believe me. No one would believe I was being molested, and no one would certainly believe this respected teacher was crushing the heart of an eight-year-old.

One day after lunch I had a pencil in my hand, waiting in line to go back to class. She walked by, and her leg caught the tip of my pencil. She immediately jerked, pulled the pencil out of my hand, whispered obscene words to me, and stomped back into class. Even though I hadn't purposely stabbed her with a pencil, I can't lie and say I didn't smile when she wasn't looking. I felt a little victorious.

There were days she would make me take my lunch to the principal's office and eat, telling the principal I was being disrespectful while telling me it was because I was too fat to eat with the other students. I would open my chocolate milk, eat my lunch, and take myself out of reality. I daydreamed I was somewhere else.

That was the year I sat at your kitchen table and heard Dolly Parton for the first time on the radio. She was singing "Silver and Gold." From that day on, her music was an escape for me. I would go home and put her *Eagle When She Flies* cassette tape in and blare it until my mom got home from work. The real world didn't exist when she was singing. I was safe when Dolly Parton was on.

There were days I had to sit in the hallway, or the principal's office depending on her mood, without lunch. Those were the days I was "too fat to eat anything." Once again, I would escape reality and get lost in the words of "Eagle When She Flies." Someday, I would fly.

> She's been there, God knows, she's been there
> She has seen and done it all
> She's a woman, she knows how to
> Dish it out or take it all
> Her heart's as soft as feathers
> Still she weathers stormy skies
> And she's a sparrow when she's broken
> But she's an eagle when she flies

Then came the day of victory for me. It was the day she would never control me again. I don't remember what I had done to set her off that day, but she was on a roll. This time it was she and I at lunch out on the playground. She looked into my eyes and told me how pathetic I was. Once again, I was reminded of how fat I was. How ugly I was. How I would never be anybody. The she ordered me to run laps around the playground.

As I ran around in circles, feeling defeated, as usual, there was nothing taking me out of my reality. There was no music to escape to. There were no daydreams to take me away from the present. Instead, my face got red, my breaths got shorter, and my legs were killing me. I could hear her yelling at me from across the playground to keep going. I started again, afraid of what she might do next. Then I stopped.

Her footsteps got swifter as she walked over to me and grabbed my face in her hands, degrading me in her Cruella Deville tone. I could feel the heat rising in my body like never before. Her words were becoming mumbled as she squeezed my cheeks harder.

The volcano erupted. I slapped her hand down, and she stared at me with her mouth wide open. As she started to point her finger toward my face and ramble on again, I opened my mouth. I was a red-faced, eight-year-old, little girl, whose anger would hide no more.

"Stop it!" I yelled. "Don't you ever talk to me like that again! Don't you ever touch me again! I hate you! You're a witch! Don't ever touch me again!" She stared at me, walked off the playground, and left me standing there. I had never felt so victorious. I was in control. I felt like I could conquer the world.

From that day forward, there was no more "Pig in the Pot." I ate lunch where everyone else ate lunch. Mrs. Baker didn't even acknowledge my existence. That was the year I became victorious. No one would molest me again. No one would hurt me again. *Ever!*

I convinced myself at that moment that in order to survive this world, I had to be in control. Being in control kept others from hurting me. I seemed to have the power in my hands, and I was going to keep it that way. The feeling of being in control didn't just stop with my authority, though. It was with everyone—friends, family, and strangers. I had it written on my heart that every single person in this world wanted to hurt me. I wasn't letting my guard down with anyone.

I was like a tiger let loose from his cage. The anger had finally come out, and I didn't know how to put it back in. I beat kids up for looking at me wrong. I made an effort not to smile unless absolutely necessary. It almost became an unspoken rule to my classmates that what happened in Mrs. Baker's class stayed in class.

Growing up in a small town with only fifty-eight students in my graduating class, I never wanted to talk about what happened. I wanted to pretend like it didn't happen. We kept it that way. They never talked about it in front of me anyway. I controlled whom I allowed to be my friends and whom I allowed to get close to me. Is the word whom correct there? The number was small. As I got older, I got along with everyone. I could make people laugh, but it usually turned ugly when you tried to get to know my heart.

I was mad at those who had sexually abused me. I was mad at Mrs. Baker. I was mad at Mom. I was mad at you. I was angry at the world. I had to be in control. To this day, that is how I have lived my life. Until I came here, very few people were allowed to get inside the walls, and even they were only allowed to a certain point.

I had no control as a child. People took control of me and forced me to do things I didn't have the power to say no to. To rebel against rules and authority has become natural for me. It scares me to do something I am told when I don't have control over it.

It makes me sad, really. I'm sad to know how much I missed out on because of my need to be in control of situations in my life. I allowed my childhood to turn me into a control freak. All this time I thought I was in control, but the truth of the matter is, I have let Mrs. Baker continue to control me. I have given that woman way too much power. But I am thrilled to know of God's redemption. He gives second chances. This next chapter in my life is going to be filled with second chances.

I do find myself wondering why you depended on alcohol and drugs so much throughout your life. Didn't it bother you not being in control? That's why drugs and alcohol has never been my favorite thing. I don't have control over who I am. Last year when I went to the emergency room because of my gallbladder, I became aware of my problem to be in control. The nurse gave me a shot of pain medication, and within a minute I was freaking out. I remember trying to sit up as I yelled, "I don't like this. I'm not in control!"

Les Parrott says in his book *The Control Freak*, "Faced with traumatic events over which they have no control, people also come to feel helpless and hopeless." I have been both. I have been an eight-year-old, helpless little girl, controlled by a manipulating teacher, and I have also been in control. The latter feels much better. Just because it feels better, though, doesn't mean it is better. Satan can make things appear to look better than they are. I think the need to be in control appears better than it really is.

Parrott also says, "Controlling too much creates as much stress as feeling that you have no control at all." That is definitely true. I was in the midst of this statement before I came to TRFC. I was working a full-time job.

I was volunteering at the church at least twenty hours per week. I was doing marketing for my chiropractor in my free time going to the gym to compete in a weight loss competition. And the week before I came here, I had signed up to go back to college. To top it all off, I was struggling with serious spiritual warfare without sleep. People kept asking me if I needed help. "I've got it under control," I would say. Yeah right!

The truth was that I was less powerful than I even imagined. I have learned at the root of control is anxiety and fear. Parrott says, "Anxiety feeds your desire to create a world that runs just the way you want it to. You know how it causes you to compulsively control not only your environment but also the people in it. You count on their compliance. You get frustrated with their needs and unhealthy attempts to control it."

I can get pretty scared when my "controlled" world changes. Sometimes it's in the big things, sometimes in the small things. I tend to get upset when my controlled environment changes. He summed me up pretty well when he said, "You can have a tough exterior, but your emotional soul can be riddled with anxiety and fear of failure."

I thought I was so tough. I guess I did a good job of pretending, for most people anyway. But inside I was desperate. I wanted so much to understand what was going on inside of me. Until recently that eight-year-old little girl was still living inside of me. I was scared to let her out. If I let her go, I would be too vulnerable. If I allowed myself to be vulnerable, I was opening the door for way too much hurt.

It's all lies! I have to risk being hurt. I wish I would have known this soon enough to teach you. I wish I could have told you in person that you had to take the risk of being hurt. Maybe you could have been vulnerable. Maybe we would have been vulnerable with each other more. I watched you go through it, too. I watched you want to be in control of your situations as well. I could never figure out why, until recently. You were scared, just like me.

I remember you telling me the story of Grandma hurting you as a kid. I actually think of it a lot. You were just a little innocent boy then. You had dreams. I bet you dreamed of Cowboys and Indians. But your reality was your parents were alcoholics. Having your own mother beat you over the head with a mirror in the bathtub quickly took your dreams away.

I wonder how different your life would have been if you wouldn't have allowed that and many other things in your life to continue to control you. You let Grandma control you, even when you thought you were in control, just like I did with Mrs. Baker. You controlled others, but really, you were just a scared little boy living inside of a grown man. Somewhere deep inside I choose to believe you wanted to be vulnerable, but you just didn't know how.

Not everyone is out to hurt me. I don't have to run from a job when my boss corrects me. I don't have to tell them how to run their company; they have it covered. I don't have to speak hurtful words to someone just because they don't agree with me. I don't have to believe that I have to hurt them before they hurt me anymore. I am overcoming my fear of disapproval. It's okay not to be in control.

Katie is teaching me this as well. I have been so controlling in my conversations with her because I couldn't understand her. I told myself what she had to say was unimportant and a waste of my time. Because of that, I would cut the conversation short or interrupt so that I could make my point clear. After all, my point was right and the *only* one that mattered; so I thought. I was ridiculous really.

I have to laugh at myself as I think back on a few things that have happened over the last nine months. I have wanted to be in control over so many things Fran has chosen to do in this program. Why? It was change. Change means hurt. Change means I am not in control. But letting my rebellion and fear well up takes the freedom of others away. Now that I look back, I am wondering how she has put up with me so long.

This is why I have had such a hard time admitting that I am wrong. Yes, I am still working on this area. However, I have to say I have made some serious progress. Instead of arguing with Fran every time she does something I disagree with, God has blessed me with a filter. I am able to think through what I'm about to say, and nine times out of ten, I simply say okay and walk away. I love that God is changing me. I think it all leads back to pride, once again. The more you swallow your pride the easier it is. It's a road straight to humility.

I want freedom in all of my relationships. I see other controlling people around me, and I don't like the way it looks on them. Usually the very things you don't like in someone else is something you see in yourself. True statement. If controlling doesn't look good on them, I'm pretty sure I don't want to wear it either. It's not my size. I'm growing out of it.

June 26, 2010

I ran a 5K today! Doctors told me I would never walk again after I broke my legs, and today, I ran 3.1 miles. Jammie was there to watch and cheer me on. I walked up to her at the end of the race, sweat running down my face, and gave her a hug. The race kind of reminded me of just how far we have come in our friendship.

We have worked through a lot of blood, sweat, and tears to get where we are today. We used to run the other way, away from our fears. But today we run against our fears. We fight to get to the finish line, knowing our friendship is worth the race.

Thank you God, for restoration. Thank you that with your strength, things are worth fighting for. Thank you for friendships that cannot be broken. It's only because of you that I can call her my sister with love and mean it.

August 14, 2010

Jammie was there the day I came here, packing my suitcase for me. She bought me this journal with a note that said, "I love you very much. Please know that I will always be there for you. You will always be my best friend." Today as I received my completion certificate, there she was. Promise kept.

Never underestimate the power of a friendship.

Stasi Eldridge asks in the book *Captivating,* "When did you first know that you were no longer a girl but had become a woman, a 'grown up'? Was there a milestone? An event?"

Tonight's completion ceremony was that moment for me. It was an event for sure. It was a milestone. And I felt captivated. I felt like a princess. I felt like a woman. I take that back. Tonight I was a woman! Who knew I would stand on a stage in a dress embraced by confidence?

I'll admit that I was seriously considering jeans and a T-shirt earlier this morning. Only five people had seen the dress. I could take it back and be done with it. The girls quickly brought me back to the reality that wouldn't be happening. Getting dressed was quite comical. Each step of the process seemed to play out in slow motion like the playback of a football game.

Let's start with the girdle—not my idea! I would like to know the thoughts behind the invention of the girdle. Did a woman just sit around one day, look down to find her gut protruding from her dress and decide she needed to suck it in? I will say this, though: I had a nice form, even though I was picking a wedgie out every five minutes.

Then there was the dress. I stood in the middle of the bedroom with my arms in the air as my friend Louanne gently placed it over my head so not to mess up my hair. I sucked in the gut even more and on went the dress. How do women do this every day without help? I'm just curious.

The shoes. The rings. The bracelets. I started to get giddy. No, this isn't the first time in my life I had worn a dress, although you could count the number of times on one hand. But this time it was different. I touched up the lipstick and we were ready to go. I will admit that I walked back to the bathroom to take a second look, just to make sure the gorgeous woman walking out that door was really me. I clean up nice. No pride intended.

Oh, how I wish you could have been there tonight. Your little girl was all grown up. I know, a twenty-six-year-old is already a grown-up, but that's not the truth. I wasn't a grown-up. One year ago I was still a scared, little girl pretending I could survive in a grown-up world. I was just surviving.

Panic started to take root when I stood in the sanctuary and got a smile from Ted B. People were going to see me! He walked up and gave me a bear hug. God must have known exactly what I needed at that moment. His hugs melt my heart and give me peace. The next best thing would have been a hug from you. I stayed in the sanctuary as long as I could before realizing that others would soon come looking for me. It was time.

I walked into the lobby of Woodland Hills Family Church to a room full of family and friends, some who hadn't seen me in over a year. It took all of about thirty seconds before the tears started streaming and the mascara started running. Last time I had seen some of these people, I was a 330-pound mess in an XXL T-shirt and size thirty jeans. Today I was in a dress, 145 pounds lighter, with Jesus all over me.

I never thought weight loss would be a reality for me. I never thought I would get to the point where I was actually ready to change. After you went into the hospital in September 2008 and I got sick that same month, I knew it was time to change. Reality had set in that no one could fix me. I had to do it myself. I couldn't wait on others anymore.

It started with that day in October 2008 when Jennifer recommended I go for a walk around the parking lot of the apartment complex. Why not go for it? I had nothing to lose. I walked. I cleared my head. I tried to understand what was happening to you, and to me. The next day I did it again. Then again.

By the time you died in February, I had lost over 40 pounds. When I came to TRFC, I had lost 90. Here I am one year later, down 55 more pounds. I never thought I would see that day in June when I actually ran a 5K. And to think it all started with a walk. Regardless of how much weight I have lost, or continue to lose, I'll always crave your fried bologna and cheese sandwich, potato soup, and barbeque.

I stood in front of the mirror this morning with a smile on my face, realizing that for the first time in my life I was completing something. Can you believe I actually made it? Sometimes I wonder how I made it this far. We'll go with option A—God!

They played a slideshow today of the last twelve months. As the pictures flew across the screen, one year of my life was narrowed down into seven minutes. Sledding, cleaning, laughing, the day the barbecue grill singed my hair, water fights, camping, playing guitar, praying. A slide show only scratches the surface of my experience there. It just brushes over a tiny corner.

It was time to speak. I stood up, fought the urge to pick my wedgie, looked into Caleb's eyes and headed toward the stage. I was completely fine. Then I looked at Tori. Before one word was spoken, I was crying. Go figure. Did I get that from you?

Through my tears I managed to blubber, "I love you. We've walked through so much together, and I love you." The tears muffled the rest of the words. Yes, I'm a crybaby.

Then I shared my story. I started with the details of my sexual abuse as a little girl. When I began to speak about the rape, I took a deep breath. This was the first time in my life that people would know this about me. I looked at Caleb, out into the audience, and back at Caleb. I was so thankful that I had prepared him for this two days prior.

That was an awkward moment, sitting down with a nine-year-old to explain some of the traumatic events that had taken place in my life.

"I want to talk to you about some things that happened to me throughout my life. I know you think the reason I am here is because my dad died and I had a sad heart, but there are other reasons, too."

"Okay." He nodded his head and waited patiently as I took a deep breath.

"Do you know what it means to be molested?"
"Yes."
"What's it mean?"
"When somebody touches you in your private places and they're not supposed to."

"That's right. When I was little girl, I had some people do that to me. I didn't tell anyone because I was scared. But now I know that wasn't the thing to do. I should have told someone. Because I held that in so long, it made me sick and very sad."

I took a brief pause to make sure it soaked in with him before I went on. He reminds me so much of me. Whether or not things faze him, he can pretend they don't. I couldn't see through him this time. I couldn't see if he was hiding emotions or if he was really okay.

"Do you know what rape means?"

He shook his head no.

"Do you know what sex is?"

"I think."

"What do you think it is?"

"It's when adults get together to make babies."

I desperately wanted to go with that answer and move on, but I felt the need to explain just a little further.

"Sex is used for that reason, but it's something that happens between married people that love each other."

I had to force myself to breathe at this point. I wiped my sweaty palms on my pant leg, clasped my hands together, and took another deep breath as Caleb laid back in the oversized chair, waiting for this conversation to continue, or get over with, I'm not sure which one. I wanted to be as calm as he looked.

"When I was a teenager, someone forced me to have sex when I didn't want to. That is called rape. I didn't tell anyone about it either, until I came here. It was another secret I kept that I shouldn't have."

I filled him in on using drugs as a teenager, confirmed my broken heart over your death, and also told him how much my heart ached when he moved away.

"Do you have any questions?"

He shook his head no, hugged me, and then found his way to the toys. I think it affected me more than it did him.

I could hear a few gasps in the audience as I discussed being raped. It took me a moment to get the words out, but once I said them, I knew I couldn't go back. I made a specific point not to make eye contact with anyone at this point. I was certainly ready to move onto the next subject.

I talked about you. It was different this time, though. There was no bitterness as I discussed your absence throughout my life. I wasn't mad at you tonight. I didn't feel abandoned. The best part of talking about you was letting them know that you took a step of faith. I had the opportunity to stand up there and confidently proclaim that I will see you again someday because you are with Jesus. I'm so proud of you for that. Not that you need my approval, but I just wanted you to know.

I talked about Grandpa dying, Caleb leaving, my food addiction, reestablishing a relationship with Mom, losing my pride, dealing with my fears, and learning how to love.

"Fran has reassured me that after standing up here tonight having completed the Table Rock Freedom Center, that my fear of success will no longer exist," I said. "I think she's right." Tonight was the end of something but just the beginning of another journey.

Lauren and I closed out the ceremony with a song I wrote that fit perfectly with the end of this journey called "Something To Offer This World."

> Verse one
> I once thought the world had something to offer me
> I searched and I searched and came up empty
> Everything I tried didn't turn out right
> Still came up void, still dying inside
>
> Chorus
> Now I've got something to offer this world
> It ain't riches it ain't fame
> Sweet simplicity, His glory I hold
> I've got something to offer this world
> I've got something to offer this world
>
> Verse two
> I've lost my way more times than I can count
> That lonely road I've traveled finally ran out
> The path I walked, oh my footsteps washed away
> My past replaced with His saving grace
>
> Repeat chorus
>
> Bridge
> I once was lost but now I'm found
> Was blind but now I see
>
> Repeat Chorus
>
> I've got something to offer this world
> I've got something to offer this world

It's true. I finally have something to offer the world. I guess I have always had it—that gift and talent that God instilled in me. I could never offer it, though, because I was too broken. Today is different. I took one last look at the crowd that had shown up to support me and said, "Today I stopped being a believer in Jesus Christ and became a follower." I walked off that stage believing it.

That was it. I would go to my parents' house and talk in my bedroom after 8:00 p.m. I would eat a snack in the living room. I would stay awake past 10:00 p.m. on a Saturday night. Is that what I took away from this last year? No. But I would be lying if I said I'm not going to enjoy it. I will go to sleep tonight in a strange place, but I will wake up to my family.

This has been one long journey. Who knew that a year ago I would be writing you letters. God has a funny way of working things out. I completed something, Dad. I really completed something. I did it for the both of us. I know it is selfish of me to say I wish that you were here, but it's the truth. I know you are right where you need to be, but sometimes I wish I could do more than just write you letters.

I can picture tonight with you here. You could have reached out your hand as I walked off the steps of the stage and taken mine. I would see the pride in your eyes as your little girl stood in a black dress in the middle of the aisle. Tonight you would have been dressed up. A suit would have been a far stretch but nice. We would have argued the week before about your outfit as you so pleasantly displayed your *Hawaii Five-O* shirt with a "What's the matter with this?" look on your face. But after a pouty lip and a little begging from me, you would have shopped for a suit. You would have done it for me. I know that now. It's picture-perfect.

I'm reminded of the day we sat in the living room and watched my high school graduation on video. I looked over at you as you watched me receive my diploma through the television screen. You were smiling, but I could see the tears you were trying to hide. I was so mad at you that I wouldn't let you come to my graduation. I still remember the day I told you on the phone. Before I hung up on you I screamed the words, "I hate you!" I stood there that day desperately hoping you were in the crowd somewhere, wishing you would go against what I said and just show up. You didn't. You respected my wishes, and I was so mad at you for it. I'm sorry. Forgive me. I'm so sorry that I didn't realize how much you were hurting, too. If take-backs really existed, that day would be top on my list.

You know, it is amazing how much I have learned about you and your heart, even though you weren't here. I know inside of you was a little boy scared, just like the little girl inside of me. I know that you were a man desperately searching for answers but couldn't find which way to go. We are so much alike. But I found the right way to go. I kept searching and reached out. That's what you were missing that I was lucky enough to find—that we had to reach out. I'll never stop reaching out.

You loved me, and I know that. You were proud of me, and I know that. You never meant to hurt me, and I know that, too. You were for me. I am going to sleep tonight with your t-shirt on and the assurance that I am still your little girl.

Maybe you did know I was a princess after all.